PROCESS THEOLOGY

PUBLISHED BY THE WESTMINSTER PRESS

BY JOHN B. COBB, JR., AND DAVID RAY GRIFFIN
Process Theology: An Introductory Exposition

BY JOHN B. COBB, JR.
Process Theology as Political Theology

Christ in a Pluralistic Age

Liberal Christianity at the Crossroads

The Theology of Altizer:
Critique and Response (Ed.)

God and the World

The Structure of Christian Existence

A Christian Natural Theology:
Based on the Thought of Alfred North Whitehead

Living Options in Protestant Theology:
A Survey of Methods

Varieties of Protestantism

BY DAVID RAY GRIFFIN
God, Power, and Evil: A Process Theodicy

A Process Christology

PROCESS THEOLOGY

An Introductory Exposition

JOHN B. COBB, JR.
and
DAVID RAY GRIFFIN

Westminster John Knox Press
LOUISVILLE • LONDON

Grateful acknowledgment is made to The Macmillan Company for
quotations from Alfred North Whitehead, *Process and Reality,*
copyright 1929 The Macmillan Company.

BOOK DESIGN BY DOROTHY E. JONES

PUBLISHED BY THE WESTMINSTER PRESS ®

PRINTED IN THE UNITED STATES OF AMERICA

16 17 18 19 20

Library of Congress Cataloging in Publication Data

Cobb, John B
   Process theology.

   Bibliography: p.
   Includes index.
   1. Process theology. I. Griffin, David,
1939–   joint author. II. Title.
BT83.6.C6   230   76–10352
ISBN 0–664–24743–1

CONTENTS

FOREWORD 7

KEY TO REFERENCES 12

1. Basic Concepts of Process Philosophy 13

2. Doctrinal Beliefs and Christian Existence 30

3. God as Creative-Responsive Love 41

4. A Theology of Nature 63

5. Human Existence 80

6. Jesus Christ 95

7. Eschatology 111

8. The Church in Creative Transformation 128

9. The Global Crisis and a Theology of Survival 143

APPENDIX A: Philosophy and Theology 159

APPENDIX B: A Guide to the Literature 162

INDEX 187

In Memory of
Daniel Day Williams

FOREWORD

This book is an introductory exposition of the theological movement that has been strongly influenced by the philosophies of Alfred North Whitehead and Charles Hartshorne. While there are some differences between the positions of these two men, they are minor in comparison with the agreements. The position they hold in common is widely known as "process philosophy" and the theological movement influenced by it is accordingly called "process theology." The term "process" rightly suggests that this movement rejects static actuality and affirms that all actuality is process. Nevertheless, it is misleading in two respects.

First, there are many other philosophies that could with equal justice be called "process philosophies." Hegel, Bergson, and Dewey are among influential modern thinkers who have stressed process in contrast with static being or substance. Second, Whitehead and Hartshorne themselves have identified their distinctive contributions with other terms. Whitehead spoke of his thought as the "philosophy of organism" to point to his understanding of the individuals of which the world is composed. Hartshorne has spoken of "societal realism" to stress that there is a plurality of real entities intimately related. He used the term "creative synthesis" in the title of his most comprehensive book to emphasize that each entity is a self-creation out of a complex many. When describing his position on God, to which he has given extended attention, he has called himself a "neo-classical theist" to indicate his relation of continuity and discontinuity with traditional theism, a "dipolar theist" to accentuate his critique of the one-sidedness of traditional theism, and a "panentheist" to indicate his view of the relation of God and the world. Nevertheless, we have retained the term "process" to identify this philosophical and theological movement simply because it does point to one chief feature of this movement, and also because it has become established usage.

Process theology speaks about God. Whitehead and Hartshorne have both used the word "God" frequently and without embarrassment. However, they have been conscious that what they have meant by the term is philosophically and religiously opposed to much that has been meant by "God" in metaphysical, theological, and popular traditions. Their use of the conventional word for unconventional purposes continues to offend many theists and atheists alike. We follow them in their usage; and we hope that the explanations in the book will show why we do so and that this practice is justified. But to make clear that many of the common connotations of the word do not fit with our meaning, we single out five in advance for rejection. Anyone who supposes that these are essential to the meaning of the word "God" will then be forewarned that we speak of a different reality. (The contrasting doctrines of process theology are explained in Chapter 3.)

1. *God as Cosmic Moralist.* At its worst this notion takes the form of the image of God as divine lawgiver and judge, who has proclaimed an arbitrary set of moral rules, who keeps records of offenses, and who will punish offenders. In its more enlightened versions, the suggestion is retained that God's most fundamental concern is the development of moral attitudes. This makes primary for God what is secondary for humane people, and limits the scope of intrinsic importance to human beings as the only beings capable of moral attitudes. Process theology denies the existence of this God.

2. *God as the Unchanging and Passionless Absolute.* This concept derives from the Greeks, who maintained that "perfection" entailed complete "immutability," or lack of change. The notion of "impassibility" stressed that deity must be completely unaffected by any other reality and must lack all passion or emotional

response. The notion that deity is the "Absolute" has meant that God is not really related to the world. The world is really related to God, in that the relation to God is constitutive of the world—an adequate description of the world requires reference to its dependence on God—but even the fact that there is a world is not constitutive of the reality of God. God is wholly independent of the world: the God-world relation is purely external to God. These three terms—unchangeable, passionless, and absolute—finally say the same thing, that the world contributes nothing to God, and that God's influence upon the world is in no way conditioned by divine responsiveness to unforeseen, self-determining activities of us worldly beings. Process theology denies the existence of this God.

3. *God as Controlling Power.* This notion suggests that God determines every detail of the world. When a loved one dies prematurely, the question "Why?" is often asked instinctively, meaning "Why did God choose to take this life at this time?" Also, when humanly destructive natural events such as hurricanes occur, legal jargon speaks of "acts of God." On the positive side, a woman may thank God for the rescue of her husband from a collapsed coal mine, while the husbands of a dozen other women are lost. But what kind of a God would this be who spares one while allowing the others to perish? Process theology denies the existence of this God.

4. *God as Sanctioner of the Status Quo.* This connotation characterizes a strong tendency in all religions. It is supported by the three previous notions. The notion of God as Cosmic Moralist has suggested that God is primarily interested in order. The notion of God as Unchangeable Absolute has suggested God's establishment of an unchangeable order for the world. And the notion of God as Controlling Power has suggested that the present order exists because God wills its existence. In that case, to be obedient to God is to preserve the status quo. Process theology denies the existence of this God.

5. *God as Male.* The liberation movement among women has made us painfully aware how deeply our images of deity have been sexually one-sided. Not only have we regarded all three "persons" of the Trinity as male, but the tradition has reinforced these images

with theological doctrines such as those noted above. God is totally active, controlling, and independent, and wholly lacking in receptiveness and responsiveness. Indeed, God seems to be the archetype of the dominant, inflexible, unemotional, completely independent (read "strong") male. Process theology denies the existence of this God.

Although all theologians acknowledging the dominant influence of Whitehead and/or Hartshorne agree in these five negations, there are important diversities among us. An "introduction to process theology" would properly require a survey of the major positions represented within the movement. In the present book we have, besides explicating some of Whitehead's basic ideas, simply spelled out our own views. For this reason we have not called this "an introduction to process theology" but "an introductory exposition."

We hope it will show the creative potentiality of a process perspective in theology to persons familiar with other approaches. We recognize that those with less academic preparation in the field may find it demanding. Readers who prefer to begin with a general orientation to the historical origins and development of process thought and to gain some understanding of the options within it before reading this particular expression of the movement are encouraged to read Appendix B.

Process theology is a form of philosophical theology. In Appendix A a brief justification is offered for this type of theology. The problem for communication of any philosophical theology is that it employs ideas and ways of thinking some of which are not familiar to the community at large. Hence, along with presenting the affirmations of the faith, a philosophical theology must introduce the distinctive modes of thought by which it hopes to illumine and enliven the self-understanding of faith. The first two chapters of this book introduce concepts derived from Whitehead's philosophy along with indications of their religious importance. These chapters unavoidably make the greatest demands on theological readers.

David Griffin wrote the first version of this Preface, Chapters 1–4, and Appendix A. John Cobb wrote the first version of Chapters 5–9. However, each has revised the work of the other. The authors consider the whole their joint project.

We wish to express our gratitude to Sharleen ("Marty") Martenas, William Beardslee, Philip Verhalen, Gordon Jackson, and Carolyn Stahl for reading the entire manuscript and making valuable suggestions, and to Lewis Ford and Barry Woodbridge for help on Appendix B. We are indebted to Mar Goman and the other secretaries at the School of Theology at Claremont for typing the manuscript quickly and competently. A special word of thanks is due to Dr. Rosino Gibellini of Editrice Queriniana, who proposed the idea of this book to us. Finally, we are grateful to Jack Keller for preparing the Index.

KEY TO REFERENCES

The following abbreviations are used to refer to the writings of Alfred North Whitehead.

AI   *Adventures of Ideas.* The Macmillan Company, 1933.

FR   *The Function of Reason.* Princeton University Press, 1929.

Imm.   "Immortality," in Paul A. Schilpp (ed.), *The Philosophy of Alfred North Whitehead.* Tudor Publishing Company, 1951. Pp. 682–700.

MT   *Modes of Thought.* The Macmillan Company, 1938.

PR   *Process and Reality.* The Macmillan Company, 1929.

RM   *Religion in the Making.* The Macmillan Company, 1926.

SMW   *Science and the Modern World.* The Macmillan Company, 1926.

1

BASIC CONCEPTS
OF PROCESS PHILOSOPHY

Whitehead noted that "whatever suggests a cosmology, suggests a religion." (*RM* 141.) Carl Becker explains the reason: "The
desire to correspond with the general harmony springs perennial
in the human breast." (*The Heavenly City of the Eighteenth-Century Philosophers* [Yale University Press, 1932], p. 63.) For this
reason Whitehead's basic philosophical ideas to be explained in this
chapter are not only background for more explicitly theological
discussions in subsequent chapters; they also have theological importance in themselves. Furthermore, since our own experiences
are instances of the reality to which these ideas apply, they are
immediately relevant to our existence as persons. They describe the
necessary and universal features of our experience and indicate the
options for self-actualization within these ontologically given
structures.

Since the ideas apply to our own experience and to all actualities
whatsoever, they gain added significance from the merging of immediate, existential relevance with metaphysical depth. Like the
categories (or *Existenzialien*) of existential philosophies, they refer
to our existence as acting, feeling, deciding, responding subjects.
But whereas existentialism sharply distinguishes human experience
from everything else, process philosophy sees it as a high-level
exemplification of reality in general. Hence the ideas for understanding human existence take on an added depth of importance.

PROCESS

Process thought by definition affirms that process is fundamental. It does not assert that *everything* is in process; for that would mean that even the fact that things are in process is subject to change. There are unchanging principles of process and abstract forms. But to be *actual* is to be a process. Anything which is not a process is an abstraction from process, not a full-fledged actuality.

The bare assertion that the actual is processive has religious significance even by itself. Since the world as we experience it is a place of process, of change, of becoming, of growth and decay, the contrary notion that what is actual or fully real is beyond change leads to a devaluation of life in the world. Since our basic religious drive is to be in harmony with the fully real, belief that the fully real is beyond process encourages one or another form of escape from full participation in the world. But to understand that the process is the reality directs the drive to be "with it" into immersion in the process.

The religious implication of reality as processive is in harmony with one of the chief consequences of the Judeo-Christian vision of reality. In this tradition, God has been viewed as active within the historical process. Accordingly, historical activity has had more importance than in traditions without a doctrine of the purposive-providential presence of the sacred reality in history. Those cultures decisively affected by the Judeo-Christian view owe to it much of their vitality.

Whitehead's view of process has a distinctive character. He affirmed that the temporal process is a "transition" from one actual entity to another. These entities are momentary events which perish immediately upon coming into being. The perishing marks the transition to the succeeding events. Time is not a single smooth flow, but comes into being in little droplets. A motion picture suggests an analogy: the picture appears to be a continuous flow, whereas in reality it is constituted by a series of distinct frames. If the process constituting our world were a single smooth flow, the boundaries of events would have to be placed upon them by perception or thought, and there would be no real individuals. All of the ideas to be developed in later sections of this chapter depend on the notion of real individuals. The boundaries of most things which are ordinarily called "events" *are* arbitrarily imposed from without, of course. Events such as elections, wars, storms, graduations, and dinners are of this type. But there are also events that have a unity of their own. As the next section will clarify further, this is an experiential unity. Events of this restricted type are true individuals. Whitehead calls them "actual occasions" or "occasions of experience."

This doctrine, that the true individuals are momentary experiences, means that what we ordinarily call individuals, the sorts of things that endure through time, are not true individuals, but are "societies" of such. Personal human existence is a "serially ordered society" of occasions of experience. In subsequent chapters this idea will frequently appear as opening up new possibilities for theological reflection.

Besides the process of transition from occasion to occasion which constitutes temporality, there is another type of process. The real individual occasions of which the temporal process is made are themselves processes. They are simply the processes of their own momentary becoming. From the external, temporal point of view they happen all at once; yet at a deeper level they are not to be understood as things that endure through a tiny bit of time unchanged, but as taking that bit of time to become. Whitehead calls this becoming "concrescence," which means becoming concrete. At this point the analogy of the motion picture breaks down, since the individual pictures are static, whereas our individual occasions of experience are dynamic acts of concrescence.

The dual emphasis on the process of transition and the process of concrescence opens the way for the understanding of a variety of religious experiences. On the one hand, transition establishes the importance of time. One occasion succeeds another. The past is composed of those events that have occurred; the future is radically different, since it contains no occasions; and the present is the occasion that is now occurring. The present is influenced by the past, and it will influence the future. Time flows asymmetrically from the past through the present into the future. There can be no denial of the reality of time nor can there be any doctrine of its circularity. Every moment is new and none can be repeated. The sense of history is undergirded. On the other hand, the experience of the "eternal now" is also intelligible. In the process of concrescence itself there is no time. This means not that there is static actuality, but that the successiveness of transition does not apply. Every moment is a now, which in this sense is timeless.

ENJOYMENT

To many people the term "process" suggests something external and objective, but for Whitehead the units of process are always as much internal as external, as much subjective as objective. They are, as stated above, "occasions of experience." In the moment of concrescence, each unit of process "enjoys" what Whitehead calls "subjective immediacy." Only when its process of concrescence is completed and hence is past does that unit of process become a datum or object for new processes to take into account.

The word "enjoy," which Whitehead frequently uses, is more suggestive than the term "process." This is both advantageous and disadvantageous. It is advantageous in that the statement that all units of process are characterized by enjoyment makes clear that every such unit has intrinsic value, an inner reality in and for itself. It is disadvantageous in that it tends to suggest connotations that cannot be attributed to all units of process, even though all are occasions of experience. Every unit of process, whether at the level of human or of electronic events, has enjoyment. Hence, we are not to think of enjoyment as being necessarily conscious, or as related to the pleasure end of the pleasure-pain continuum. What we normally mean by pleasure is bound up not only with consciousness but with the whole structure of high-grade animal bodies. But we can distinguish in this rich matrix of meaning an element that can be broadly generalized. To be, to actualize oneself, to act upon others, to share in a wider community, is to enjoy being an experiencing subject quite apart from any accompanying pain or pleasure. In Whitehead's words, experience is the "self-enjoyment of being one among many, and of being one arising out of the composition of many." (*PR* 220.) In this sense, every individual unit of process enjoys its own existence.

These units of enjoyment are not to be contrasted with some other kind of *actual* entities that lack enjoyment. To lack enjoyment would be to be a mere object, what Whitehead calls a "vacuous actuality." Whitehead rejects the notion of "vacuous actuality, void of subjective experience" (*PR* 253), and thereby rejects a (Cartesian) dualism of experiencing and nonexperiencing actualities.

All experience is enjoyment. To be actual is to be an occasion of experience and hence an occasion of enjoyment. In Whitehead's words, "the experience enjoyed by an actual entity" is "what the actual entity is in itself, for itself." (*PR* 81.) But the term "experience" also needs clarification. In many circles, experience has been equated with consciousness, whereas in other circles consciousness is seen as a high-grade form of experience. Sigmund Freud likened consciousness to the tip of an iceberg. Process thought accepts this latter view. In Whitehead's words: "Consciousness presupposes experience, and not experience consciousness." (*PR* 83.) All actualities experience, but only a few experiences rise to the level of consciousness. Even in experiences in which consciousness is attained, consciousness lights up elements which had already been unconsciously experienced in the concrescence. Further, only a small portion of the experienced ingredients is thus illumined. Consciousness is thus a selective activity. It gives special importance to a few out of the indefinite number of factors in experience. It can thereby increase the enjoyment of experience.

One qualification should be made of the comparison of consciousness with the tip of the iceberg. While consciousness only emerges as a special element in experience, it does not leave the more basic elements unchanged. The moment of experience is a self-determining whole; every factor is conditioned by all the others.

In Chapter 4 we will show how this initially startling notion, that every level of actuality enjoys experience, makes sense of the ordinary objects of experience, such as rocks, which certainly do not appear to have experiences. Also we will show how it can make sense of the idea that divine providential activity has been instrumental in the evolution of our world. Here we will only indicate one important religious implication of this notion.

The widespread modern sense of being estranged or alienated from reality is related to the dualistic view that human beings are totally different in kind from the rest of the world. For example, in the earlier phenomenological writings of Heidegger the sense of our being "thrown" into the world is closely related to the conviction that we, who "care," are in the midst of a world that does not "care." Hence, the dualistic assumption is present, even though the phenomenological method is not supposed to involve any speculations about what other things are in themselves. Likewise, in Sartre's earlier writings the sense of "nausea" is closely related to the distinction between being (that which is merely *en-soi,* or in-itself) and the human reality (that which is *pour-soi,* or for-itself). Whitehead, like Teilhard, holds that all actualities have an inner reality as well as an outer one. Hence, the sense of kinship with all things, which has evidently characterized human experience at most times and places, is rationally supported. If accepted at the level of conscious judgment, it may again gradually become accepted at the deeper levels of our experience.

ESSENTIAL RELATEDNESS

There is no one-to-one correlation between the notion of actuality as process and of actuality as enjoyment. At least some of the processes constituting actuality could be supposed to be nonexperiential. Likewise, one could suppose that enjoyment could be nonprocessive; at least traditional theists have claimed that the notion of God as immutable experience is not strictly self-contradictory (although they have admitted that it is a difficult notion, for which we have no analogical basis in our immediate experience). Nevertheless, the notions that the actualities are processes and that they consist of the enjoyment of experience do support each other.

The same is true of the relation between the notions of process and essential relatedness. It would be possible, as Leibniz has shown, to construct a philosophy in which the actualities were processes and yet were totally unrelated to each other. And much of the history of philosophy concerns the attempt to understand how substances which are essentially unchanging can have relations. However, as the difficulties in these two contrary approaches suggest, the notions of process and essential relatedness do tend to support each other. If the actual things are thought to be static, relations are nuisances, required only by the need to give the philosophy some relevance to the world as experienced; and if things have real relations with each other, and these relations belong to their respective essences, it is difficult to understand how these essences can be unchanging.

Whitehead saw that the mutual implications of process and relatedness requires that actual entities are strictly individual events. They do not endure through time. They arise, become, and reach completion. When the becoming is completed, they are then in the past; the present is constituted by a new set of occasions coming into being. The past actualities are still describable as processive and experiential, in the sense of *having been* experiencing processes; but their moment of experiencing and becoming is past. They do not endure from the past into the present and on into the future. Whitehead chooses the term "occasions of experience" partly to stress this characteristic of actual individuals. The things that endure are series of these occasions of experience. Electrons, molecules, and cells are examples of such enduring things. Likewise the human soul, or stream of experience, is composed of a series of distinct occasions of experience.

But to say that the experiences are distinct is not to say that they are independent and separable. On the contrary, a momentary experience is essentially related to previous experiences. In fact, it begins as a multiplicity of relations, and achieves its individuality through its reaction to and unification of these relations. It is not first something in itself, which only secondarily enters into relations with others. The relations are primary. Whitehead's technical terms for these relations are "prehension" and "feeling." The present occasion "prehends" or "feels" the previous occasions. The present occasion is nothing but its process of unifying the particular prehensions with which it begins.

The idea that the experiencing processes are momentary is the basic difference of Whitehead's philosophy from that of Leibniz. Like Whitehead, Leibniz saw the actual world as composed exhaustively of experiencing processes. These "monads" did not, however, experience anything beyond themselves. Although Leibniz used the term "perception" to describe their activity, he defined this perception as projection. The monads did not really enter into each other's experiences. Each one was completely "windowless," with no opening for the outside world to enter. The projected perceptions were accurate only because of a harmony between projections and external reality preestablished by Leibniz' deistic God at creation. The denial of real relatedness between the monads was seen as necessary by Leibniz in part because his monads were enduring substances with essential attributes. The essential attributes defined the identity of the substances. The rejection of openings to outside influences was necessary to protect this identity.

Each of Whitehead's occasions of experience begins, as it were, as an open window to the totality of the past, as it prehends all the previous occasions (either immediately or mediately). Once the rush of influences enters in, the window is closed, while the occasion of experience forms itself by response to these influences. But as soon as this process is completed, the windows of the world are again open, as a new occasion of experience takes its rise. Hence, the next molecular occasion within that series constituting the enduring molecule, or the next moment of human experience within that stream of experiences constituting the soul, is open to the contributions that can be received from others. In such a stream of occasions, a "defining essence" of that stream may arise, representing the characteristics that apply to each member of the stream. But this enduring stream with its stable essence is an abstraction in comparison with the individual occasions themselves, which alone are fully concrete individuals. Hence, the recognition that a molecule or a person has an enduring character—one that can remain the same in different environments—is not

prejudicial to a recognition that relations with the environment are
of the essence of fully concrete individuals.

The religious significance of the difference between these two
views is paramount. Leibniz' view reflects the traditional notion
that essential independence is a characteristic to be prized. To an
important degree this reflects the influence of the classical notion
of deity upon ideas of the world. Since God was said to be totally
independent, with no real relations to any other actualities, it was
natural to think in similar terms of the worldly actualities that God
created, especially since some of them were said to be made in the
divine image. Accordingly, the Leibnizian monads were totally
independent of everything else, except God. On this point Leibniz
is at one with Descartes, who had defined a substance (that is, a
"really real" thing) as "that which requires nothing but itself to
exist." Descartes first said that there were three kinds of substances: God, finite minds, and finite bodies. But then he pointed
out that the finite minds and bodies were not substances in the
strict sense of the term, since they did require God as their creator.
But, with this one qualification, they were as self-sufficient as God.
Given our religious drive to correspond with the really real, and
to accentuate those dimensions of our existence which we perceive
as connecting us with the depths of reality, it is not surprising that
Western culture in the past few centuries has been characterized
by an increase in atomic individualism and isolation. Even though
there have been various forms of reaction against the ideal of
self-sufficiency, the notion of "independence" by and large still
seems to evoke more religious passion than that of "interdependence."

Whiteheadian process thought gives primacy to interdependence as an ideal over independence. Of course, it portrays interdependence not simply as an ideal but as an ontologically given
characteristic. We cannot escape it. However, we can either exult
in this fact or bemoan it. Also, interdependence is a variable. We
can actualize ourselves in such a way as either to increase or
decrease it. Chapter 7 shows that the perfection of human life
involves maximizing our relatedness to others, and hence our dependence upon them. There is a distinction to be made: On the one

hand, ethical independence as a characteristic of ourselves as enduring persons is still a positive idea. That is, it is good not to be swayed from ethical principles by shifting circumstances. On the other hand, our concrete moments of experience are richer to the extent that they include others and are thereby dependent upon them. Our enjoyment emerges out of its inclusion of the enjoyments of our predecessors. They contribute to our enjoyment out of their own enjoyments. To the extent that we are open to these contributions, we will enjoy existence more deeply, and will have more to contribute to future actualities.

The Biblical tradition was an important factor in the rise of personal individuality. But it does not support the extreme individualism of the modern Western world. In it, God is not viewed as devoid of relations to the world, and in human existence primary importance is given to one's relations with God and other humans. Humans are understood as essentially belonging to a community. Process thought supports the relational, communal thrust of the Biblical view of God and humanity while extending this to include the rest of the world.

INCARNATION

Closely related to the notion that the processes of enjoyment which constitute the actual world are essentially related is the notion that they are related to each other incarnationally. The past experiences are incorporated into the present experience. To prehend a past experience is to include it. Two qualifications must be made. First, the past experience is not fully incorporated in the present one. The inclusion is selective and limited. Second, the present experience does not include the past as still experiencing. The past is present as *having been* an experience, as an experience that *was* enjoyed.

Memory is the most immediate example of the incarnation of the past in the present, and of the two qualifications. In remembering a past experience, our present experience includes, as part of its content, that past experience. We do not include the totality of that past experience, with its indefinite complexity, but only a portion of it—some of its content, and some of its subjective reaction to that content. And we do not include that past experience as still experiencing. That moment of experience is over. We may now, in recalling that past experience, feel the same emotion we felt then. But this is a new feeling of the same emotion, not that past feeling continuing to feel in the present. In other words, the past experience is in the present experience objectively, not subjectively. It is present as the object of the present subject's experience, not subjectively in the sense of still experiencing. Whitehead calls this existence of the past in the present the "objective immortality" of the past. The past is not nothing; it lives on. But it lives on objectively, as objectified by and hence incarnated in the present.

There are many dimensions to the religious significance of this doctrine. First, as the phrase "objective immortality" itself suggests, this doctrine is relevant to our desire to have our experiences make a lasting difference and in fact to live on beyond themselves. The relativity definition of the past and future is incorporated into process thought: the past is the totality of that which influences the present, and the future is the totality of that which will be influenced by the present. This implies, on the one hand, that each occasion is a selective incarnation of the whole past universe. It implies, on the other hand, that our activities will make a difference throughout the future. Future occasions will necessarily prehend us. The doctrine of influence as incarnation implies that we will be objectively immortal.

Second, this doctrine means that efficient causation, which is the causation of one actuality upon another, is by means of incarnation in the other. We influence each other by entering into each other. This contrasts with the view of efficient causation that has dominated the modern world, the notion that the cause is completely external to the effect. This prevailing view is closely related, of course, to the notion of actualities as essentially independent of each other. The model for causation has been that of essentially independent billiard balls bouncing off each other. The balls are related, and produce changes in each other; but the relations and the resulting changes are purely "accidental," i.e., they do not enter into the essences of the balls.

This notion has been another one of the many conceptual strands behind the ecological crisis. We have had the view that the ultimate constituents of the world were like tiny billiard balls. Any changes brought about in the world involved only the rearrangement of externally related bits of matter. Since they did not permeate each other, no irreversible changes could be effected. If some combination of things is found to have unfortunate consequences, the combination can simply be undone, and things will be returned to the state they were in before. Ecology, as the study of the interrelationships of things, has taught us that this view is false. Interrelations are internal to things. Whitehead's thought is thoroughly ecological. It involves extending to the status of a universal truth Paul's insight that we are "members of one another." This will be discussed further in Chapter 4.

The notion that the causation between two actualities involves the incarnation of the cause into the effect also has obvious relevance to the question of how God influences the world in general, and of how God was related to Jesus in particular. This will be discussed in Chapter 6.

CREATIVE SELF-DETERMINATION

Thus far, most of what has been said would be compatible with a deterministic universe. We have stressed that the processes of enjoyment arise out of their feelings or prehensions of other such processes, and then contribute some of their feelings to future occasions of experience. The emphasis has been on their dependence, not on their autonomy, upon efficient causation, not final causation. And, though little has been said yet about the world's relation to God, the above notions would seem compatible with the traditional view of the world as creation.

However, this one-sided emphasis gives a false picture of process thought. Equally essential is the notion that the processes of enjoyment are partially self-creative. The world is indeed creation, as Chapter 4 will stress; but it is also creative. Each occasion of experience begins as a reception of a multitude of influences from the past. This relatedness to the past belongs to the essence of the present individual. It must take account of its past, and this past sets boundaries determining what is possible for the present individual. However, precisely how the present subject responds to its past, precisely how it incorporates the past feeling, precisely how it integrates the multiplicity of feelings into a unified experience—this is not determined by the past. The past does not dictate precisely how it will be immortalized. This is determined by each present actuality. For each actuality is partially self-creative; it finally creates itself out of the material that is given to it.

In other words, after the influences from the environment have given birth to it, the occasion of experience takes control of its own existence, completing what others had started. Final causation finishes what efficient causation had begun. "Final causation" is the power of the end or purpose. The purpose of every occasion of experience is enjoyment of an appropriate kind. The aim of the present occasion of experience is first of all to create an enjoyable experience for itself out of the available materials.

This doctrine of the partial self-determination of every actuality reconciles efficient and final causation, real influence with real freedom. Some views, in order to protect freedom, have denied genuine causal influence between actualities. But the notion of efficient causation is also important religiously. Without it, there would be no basis for either gratitude or our sense of responsibility for the consequences of our actions. Other views have been so overwhelmed with the sense of dependence that they deny that we have anything to do with the kinds of beings we become. These views equally undercut the basis both for gratitude and for responsibility. Recognizing the equal necessity of efficient causation and self-determination, some have suggested that we need to affirm the paradox that we are totally determined and yet that we are free. Whitehead allows us to conceive both freedom and efficient causation without contradiction.

This recognition that we are partially created by our environment and partially self-created is, when conjoined with the notion that we are essentially characterized by enjoyment, of religious significance for the notion of "liberation." On the one hand, the fact that the quality of an individual's enjoyment is partly a function of that individual's total environment means that, if we are concerned with promoting the enjoyment of others, we cannot neglect the quality of their environment. In fact, no neat line can be drawn between the individual and its environment, since what is "the environment" in one moment essentially enters into the individual in the next moment. On the other hand, the fact that the individual is also essentially self-creative means that no amount of success in improving an environment can *guarantee* that an individual's enjoyment will be enhanced. The most we can do is seek to provide an optimum environment, which heightens the probability that the enjoyment will be enhanced.

This is also true of God. The divine reality so relates itself to us as to heighten the probability that enjoyment will be enhanced. But God does not compel us to enjoy. The individual experience finally determines, within the limits made possible by God and the world, what enjoyment it will realize.

Although God's role is in this way like that of other aspects of the environment, it also has its uniqueness. The aim at enjoyment is not simply one among many aspects of an experience. It is the one element in terms of which the entity achieves its unity. This aim is not derived from the past world, for it is unique to the new occasion. The occasion chooses its own "subjective aim." Still it does not make this choice in a vacuum. The attractive possibility, the lure, in relation to which its act of self-determination is made, is derived from God. This lure is called the "initial aim." God is the divine Eros urging the world to new heights of enjoyment.

Creative Self-Expression

The doctrine that every occasion of experience aims at its own self-creation points to only one half of its creative aim. Equally essential is the occasion's aim to pervade the environment, i.e., to be creative of the future. The vision involved in this aim may be negligible—the aim may be only a blind urge to perpetuate a particular form of enjoyment into the next fraction of a second. But, however negligible, the aim to express oneself is universal. Like the aim at self-creation, the aim at self-expression is final causation, but it is also the anticipation of oneself as sharing in the creation of the future, and hence as an efficient cause. Accordingly, an occasion of experience in creating itself does not aim solely at its own private enjoyment; it also aims to create itself in such a way as to make a definite contribution to the enjoyment of others.

There are several religious implications of this doctrine. First, it means that absolute egoism is ontologically ruled out. No actuality is concerned solely with itself. Second, the fact that the concern for the future is a variable means that it can be enlarged and strengthened. This is the function of morality, which is, therefore, important for the achievement of God's purposes in the world.

A third implication is that, in order to maximize the possibilities for the enjoyment of actuality, the "environment" in the sense of the conditions out of which an occasion of experience arises is not the only relevant factor. Also important is the anticipated reception of the occasion's expression of itself. That is, it is important that the occasion expect the world to be positively receptive of what it contributes. The anticipation that it will be largely ignored decreases its own enjoyment. Likewise, the anticipation that its free self-expression will lead to reprisals against others for whom it cares (including its own future experiences) will tend to inhibit this self-expression, and thereby inhibit its enjoyment.

NOVELTY

The previous two sections, dealing with creativity, have shown that present processes are not completely determined by past ones. The present experience decides, in terms of its simultaneous aim at its own enjoyment and at its self-expression beyond itself, precisely how to incorporate the elements available to it. It might be thought that this creative response merely involves a modified arrangement of elements already realized in the past, but this is not the whole truth. Novel elements, previously unactualized in the world, are also incorporated.

Every event involves the actualization of innumerable possibilities. These actualized possibilities are contained in one of two basic ways. They can either be part of the "objective content" of a feeling, i.e., *what* is felt. Or they can qualify the "subjective form" with which this content is felt, i.e., *how* it is felt. A present occasion of experience arises out of previous occasions. The possibilities which they actualized can be re-actualized by it. The possibilities that were contained as their objective content can be actualized as its own content; and the new occasion can feel this content with the same subjective form. Furthermore, what was the *how* of feeling in a past occasion, the subjective form, can be the *what* of a present feeling, the objective datum. For example, if one remembers apprehending something or someone with the subjective form of anger or of love, one can now objectify anger or love as part of the content of one's present experience. This is already a type of novelty, that a possibility which previously showed up in a subjective reaction is now in the objective content of an experience.

But there is a more radical kind of novelty. Possibilities that were never actualized in one's past can be actualized. At first glance this seems to limit the principle which process thought otherwise accepts, that all of the possibilities in an actuality arise by means of prehending other actualities. However, the principle is in fact maintained. The possibilities that were previously unactualized in the world are derived from the divine experience. One aspect of God is a primordial envisagement of the pure possibilities. They are envisaged with appetition that they be actualized in the world. The actualization of novel possibilities generally increases the enjoyment of experience; for the variety of possibilities that are actualized in an experience adds richness to the experience, and the element of novelty lends zest and intensity of enjoyment.

This means that the divine reality is understood to be the ground of novelty. This stands in tension with most religious philosophies, according to which deity (if it be the ground of anything in the world) is the ground of an established order. The God of process thought is also the ground of order, but this is a changing and developing order, an order that must continually incorporate novelty if it is not to become repressive of enjoyment. The positive appraisal of novelty resulting from this vision pervades process theology.

GOD-RELATEDNESS

What has been said of the divine incarnation in the world, the derivation from God of the initial aim toward enjoyment, and God as the organ of novelty, shows that our prehension of God is an essential part of all experience. There are not actual entities that first are self-contained and then have accidental relations to God. God-relatedness is constitutive of every occasion of experience. This does not restrict the freedom of the occasion. On the contrary, apart from God there would be no freedom. If we could think at all of a world apart from God, it would be a world of repetition lapsing into lesser and lesser forms of order according to the principle of entropy. What happened in each occasion could only be the declining outgrowth of what had happened before. It is God who, by confronting the world with unrealized opportunities, opens up a space for freedom and self-creativity.

And, far from sanctioning the status quo, recognition of essential relatedness to *this* God implies a continual creative transformation of that which is received from the past, in the light of the divinely received call forward, to actualize novel possibilities. Although this divine power is persuasive rather than controlling, it is nevertheless finally the most effective power in reality. In Whitehead's words: "The pure conservative is fighting against the essence of the universe." (*AI* 354.)

2

❦

DOCTRINAL BELIEFS
AND CHRISTIAN EXISTENCE

Chapter 1 showed that Whitehead's analysis of basic features of reality has religious implications congenial to Christian faith. These features characterize all human experience at its prereflective (prethematized) level. This chapter considers the significance of the recognition of this prereflective experience for Christian doctrine. The four sections of this discussion deal with (1) the desirability that doctrine conform with prethematized experience, (2) the inevitability of selective emphasis introduced by doctrine, (3) the implication of these ideas for the grounds for belief, and (4) the relation of Christian doctrine to history.

DOCTRINE AND
PRETHEMATIZED EXPERIENCE

Doctrine is a form given to consciously held beliefs. Such beliefs are derived from induction, deduction, and authority, as well as from immediate experience, and there is great diversity among them. Belief at this level must be distinguished from the complex of prereflective beliefs that we all hold in common, since we all immediately apprehend a common reality in every moment of our experience. These deeper beliefs are originally preconscious and prereflective. They may or may not emerge into conscious awareness.

One's conscious beliefs may conflict with what is "known" to be true at the prereflective level. For example, that the present is causally influenced (not simply preceded) by the past is universally experienced and belongs to the prereflective knowledge of all people. But some thinkers have been convinced by argument that there is no such causation. Their doctrine is that there is no meaning of "efficient causation" other than "constant conjunction," i.e., that events of type B are always preceded by events of type A. But, no matter how long and how sincerely the person holds this belief at the conscious level, the experience of causation as real influence cannot be effaced. The same holds for such other elements of prereflective experience as self-determination and God-relatedness.

This raises the question as to whether doctrines, as consciously formulated beliefs, are important. It is now widely agreed that "saving faith," the kind of faith that alone can bring wholeness, is primarily a matter of the basic emotions, attitudes, and commitments from which one's behavior follows. That is, faith is fundamentally a mode of existence. Beliefs are important only to the extent that they support this mode of existence. If all people necessarily believe in God at the deepest level of their being, even when they consciously affirm atheism, why is it important for us to reflect about our God relatedness? Are not conscious beliefs about God at best a redundant duplication of our prereflective faith, and at worst an ineffectual attempt to deny it?

The recognition of a prereflective level of knowledge, which includes knowledge of deity, does relativize the importance of conscious beliefs. The elements of this prereflective knowledge affect our attitudes, emotions, and behavior, regardless of what we consciously believe. To return to the example of causality: those who verbally deny any necessary connection between one event and its predecessors reveal in every moment that they know otherwise. They have emotions, such as guilt and anger, which presuppose real influence. They have attitudes about responsibility which likewise presuppose that some events influence others, so that the latter would not have happened without the former. And their outer actions can only be understood on the assumption that they know that these actions will have consequences which can be anticipated with some degree of probability. Hence, whether we consciously believe in efficient causation or not, our total life-stance will still reflect our prereflective knowledge of its reality. Our conscious beliefs do not efface this knowledge and its consequences for our attitudes, emotions, and decisions.

The same holds for our experience of deity. We all know, at the prereflective level, that there is a sacred reality, whose existence is supremely valuable, and that our lives finally have meaning because of our relation to this holy reality. This knowledge conditions the emotions, attitudes, and actions even of those who affirm atheism and nihilism. Further, we all feel an impulse to be the best we can in each moment, and to contribute the most we can to the future. This is reflected in the lives even of those who consciously reject all teleological notions, all ideas of objective values, and all moral principles. Hence, it is not only our prereflective faith in God and the value of life that cannot be effaced but also the effects of God's activity on us. The *Holy* Spirit in the universe has its impact upon our mode of existence, whether or not we consciously believe in it.

Hence, there is much truth in the widespread denial that our "salvation" depends upon the affirmation of true doctrines. There is no one-to-one correspondence between our conscious beliefs and our affective-volitional orientation. The basic structure of reality will impose itself upon us regardless of our conscious beliefs, and it will extract a measure of appropriate response from us. Conscious beliefs are not all-controlling.

The recognition of the primacy of prereflective experience sometimes leads to the conclusion that consciously held beliefs or doctrines are unimportant. This would follow if one's emotions, attitudes, and actions were influenced by one's conscious beliefs only slightly, or not at all. These consciously held beliefs would then be virtually or completely "epiphenomenal," that is, nonefficacious by-products of some other dimension(s) of experience.

We are sometimes led to think of conscious beliefs in this way by the great inconsistency observed between avowed opinions and actual practice. Whitehead was fully aware of this, but he saw ideas as having a force of their own such that, once they have been consciously accepted, they work toward their own fuller embodiment. He shows how the doctrine that all human beings are en-souled arose among the Greeks in barely recognized tension with the accepted institution of slavery. The doctrine survived and was assimilated into Christianity, where it gradually heightened the sense of the inappropriateness of slavery. "Finally, the humanitarian movement of the eighteenth century, combined with a religious sense of the kinship of men, has issued in the settled policy of the great civilized governments to extirpate slavery from the world." (*AI* 35.)

Fortunately, ideas in general do not have to wait two thousand years to show their effectiveness. Each individual moment of experience involves a complex mutual adjustment of its aspects, and consciously held beliefs play their part in this adjustment. Beliefs about matters of ultimate concern held with deep conviction over a long period are particularly efficacious in shaping one's character, purposes, and general emotional-attitudinal-behavioral stance. In Whitehead's words:

> A religion, on its doctrinal side, can thus be defined as a system of general truths which have the effect of transforming character when they are sincerely held and vividly apprehended. In the long run, your character and your conduct of life depend on your intimate convictions. (*RM* 15.)

In this sense doctrine has a certain priority in the Christian life. This claim needs clarification. First, the priority of conscious beliefs is not genetic. As stated in Chapter 1, consciousness is a derivative element in experience, not its foundation. In each moment of experience, one's emotions, purposes, valuations, and pre-conscious awareness of the outer world are genetically prior to the emergence of any conscious judgments. However, a moment of experience is an atomic totality, in which there is a mutual sensitivity among all the elements. This means that the emergence of consciousness is not a merely superficial addition which leaves the other elements unaffected. Just as the quality and content of consciousness is conditioned by the other elements, these other elements—the emotions, purposes, and valuations—are themselves conditioned by the emergence of conscious beliefs.

Second, the fact that human experience is constituted by a series of atomic moments of experience, and that consciousness emerges, if at all, as a derivative element in these discrete moments, does not mean that consciousness lacks cumulative effect. The data from which a moment of human experience emerges include the previous moments of the person's experience in which consciousness was an important factor. Hence, the emotions, purposes, and valuations with which a moment of experience begins may well be derived most importantly from previous *conscious* beliefs, valuations, purposes, and emotions. It is for this reason that, in the long run, the individual's affective attitudinal-purposive-behavioral stance in life can be dominantly influenced by his or her conscious judgments.

If we combine these considerations with the previous discussion of the ineradicable prereflective knowledge of reality, we see that conscious beliefs are neither all-determining nor epiphenomenal. This makes the content of such beliefs peculiarly important; for to the extent that our conscious beliefs are in tension with the universal features of human experience, we are split within ourselves. We do not experience psychic wholeness, since our emotions, valuations, and purposes and consequently our behavior are informed by conflicting beliefs. For the sake of psychic wholeness and consistency of action, it is important for our conscious beliefs to correspond with the prereflective beliefs involved in our primordial experience.

THE SELECTIVE EMPHASIS OF DOCTRINES

Conscious beliefs are important because their conformation to our prereflective knowledge affects psychic health. They are important also because those beliefs which conform to the universal depths of experience introduce selection and emphasis. This is not to be deplored; selectivity and emphasis are essential to any ordered experience, and hence to any experience whatsoever.

The preconscious apprehension of reality is indefinitely complex. The analysis of it could in principle never be exhaustive, for each experience involves, in some way and to some degree, however negligible, the totality of actuality and ideality. Consciousness focuses upon a small portion of experience. This focusing grants special importance to selected elements, which can be *consciously* valued and become influential in *conscious* decision-making.

While it is true that there are universally experienced features of reality, and that at least some of these are matters of religious significance, people in differing contexts (e.g., religious traditions) do not consciously experience the same elements. Explicitly formulated beliefs focus our attention upon certain elements in our experience, helping us become consciously aware of them. It is true that mere second-hand beliefs, i.e., those accepted upon the authority of others, are often not very influential upon one's life. But ideas that are initially received from others can become first-hand beliefs. They can lead us to perceive consciously a factor in our experience that otherwise might never have emerged into our conscious awareness. Here, too, causality is a case in point. There was a time when causal influence was not consciously noticed; but once this aspect of experience was pointed out in language, it was readily and consciously recognized.

The same point holds with respect to morality. It is based upon an impulse to moral activity that is universal. But this element is more important in some traditions than in others, and for some individuals within a given tradition than for others within the same tradition. The impulse to moral activity is more important in the lives of those people who consciously believe that moral activity is important in the scheme of things, and that there is a basis beyond themselves for the moral feelings which they do have. The existence in which moral factors are central is a different existence from that in which they are peripheral.

Out of the infinitely complex welter of elements making up human experience, metaphysical and moral teachings lift some into consciousness and thereby into increased effectiveness. The total existence of human beings is thus profoundly affected by what they believe. Those Christian doctrines which are explications of universal aspects of experience have importance in the same way. For example, they lift into consciousness certain aspects of the universal experience of deity, such as divine grace. The reality of a primordial prethematic apprehension that includes divine grace does not reduce the importance of thematization, for by itself this apprehension of grace is merely an abstraction within the total stream of experience. Christian doctrine, by selecting certain features of experience for conscious emphasis, shapes attitudes, purposes, and commitments, and even the structure of human existence itself.

PREREFLECTIVE EXPERIENCE
AND THE GROUNDS FOR BELIEF

That much of Christian doctrine is selective description of features of universal prereflective experience has implications for the justification of theological affirmations. When one no longer finds it possible to accept religious doctrines that claim to be universal truths simply because some supposedly authoritative person, book, or institution proclaims them, one is inclined to ask for proof. But what kind of proof can there be? Some ask for historical facts that provide proof, but no historical event can in itself prove any general truth. Some ask for rational proof, but every argument finally presupposes some beliefs that must be simply taken as self-evidently true.

The relevance of the universally experienced prereflective elements here becomes apparent. We apprehend more than we are able to express in language. In Whitehead's words: "Mothers can ponder many things in their hearts which their lips cannot express. These many things, which are thus known, constitute the ultimate religious evidence, beyond which there is no appeal." (*RM* 65.)

Religious doctrines claiming universal validity are to be accepted, if at all, because of their self-evidence. In Whitehead's words again: "Religion collapses unless its main positions command immediacy of assent." (*SMW* 274.) Referring to these doctrines as self-evidently true does not mean that they are equally obvious to everyone. To the contrary. The ability to perceive the previously unformulated factors in experience is extremely rare. As Whitehead says, we are not all on the same level in this regard. (*RM* 121.) The point is that, once someone has perceived them consciously and expressed them verbally, they can then be recognized by others. Whitehead uses the analogy of the tuning fork and the piano. The note on the tuning fork elicits a response from the piano, but only because the piano has a string tuned to the same note. (*RM* 128.) The verbal expression of a universally experienced fact elicits a believing response in us because we had already apprehended the fact. *(Ibid.)* The expression in verbal form simply helps us raise this apprehension into the clarity of consciousness, and hence to make it possible for this apprehended element to become more important in our lives. (*RM* 132.) It might even become *the* central element around which the other elements would become organized.

Accordingly, theology should not primarily be argumentation. It should primarily be the attempt to state the basic tenets of one's faith in such a way as to elicit a responsive perception of these as self-evidently true. This does not mean that there is no place for argument. The perception of the truth of an idea may be aided, for example, by seeing the absurd conclusions entailed in its rejection. But the argumentation should remain secondary to the attempt so to formulate beliefs that they can be immediately perceived as true.

There is another positive implication of the position taken above. If Christian doctrines are relatively adequate explications of truths that are universally apprehended at the preconscious level of experience, and if these doctrines lift into importance a selection of the myriad precognitive apprehensions, is it not likely that the same is true of the doctrines of other religious traditions? If so, should not the Christian faith of the future attempt to incorporate these other consciously apprehended truths into itself? Is this not one of the major possibilities for achieving progress in truth, which consists in "evolving notions which strike more deeply into the root of reality"? (*RM* 127.) We believe that it is possible for faith to broaden and enrich itself in this way without losing its Christian character, and that this is desirable. In fact, Christian faith itself requires this self-universalizing, once the real possibility for it is present. Subsequent chapters will make illustrative moves in this direction. But because of the breadth, complexity, and subtlety of the issues involved, this is mainly a task for the future.

Doctrine and History

Much of Christian doctrine is a description of prethematized universal experience, providing emphasis upon selected features. But this does not reduce the importance of history for Christian faith. It has been through a particular history that the selection and emphasis have fallen as they have, so that both Christian doctrine and the Christian existence it forms are inseparable from their history. The same is true for the other great Ways of humanity.

The importance of history for doctrine is especially clear in language. Words and phrases do not have a one-to-one correlation with aspects of prereflective experience. All language introduces the note of interpretation. This interpretation is shaped by the history of the language, including the speculative thought, that belongs to that history. Even our most strenuous efforts at neutral description are stamped by the history that forms us. This is simply one manifestation of the dual truth of efficient causation and self-determination. Because of the human capacity for self-determination, different human beings can respond to identical features of reality in differing ways. Because of the power of efficient causation, each of these interpretative responses can start a tradition of interpretation of reality, what Whitehead calls a "community of intuition." (*RM* 128.) The "primary expression" of the intuition by the founder elicits a "responsive expression" of that intuition in the followers. (*RM* 128–129.) Furthermore, because of the continuing reality of both efficient causation and self-determination, each stage in the various traditions can result in even further divergences from the others. The dominant language at any stage in a tradition reflects that tradition's interpretation of reality and also instills and continually reinstills that interpretation. Accordingly, the language of a tradition and the central doctrines that reflect and support that language are the prime determinants of the particular mode of existence characterizing that tradition.

Furthermore, as human existence is shaped in specialized ways during the course of history, experiences occur that are not possible to persons shaped by other traditions. For example, those shaped by a long participation in Hindu yoga or Buddhist meditation report experiences that are not merely selective emphases within prethematized universal experience. They are attainable by Westerners, if at all, only by long submission to unaccustomed psychic disciplines. Similarly, there are Christian doctrines that do not have immediate resonance among Easterners because they describe subtleties of experience that emerge only where the Western emphasis on personal freedom and divine grace has profoundly shaped human existence. In regard to these doctrines, the tuning-fork analogy only applies to people standing within the particular tradition expressing the doctrines.

This point is rooted in the distinction that Whitehead makes between abstract and real possibility. There are abstract possibilities which are possible in principle to all human beings. That is, there is nothing in the definition of "human being" which excludes the actualization of those possibilities. But not all of these things are really possible to every human being. There is an order among the abstract possibilities, so that certain ones cannot be actualized prior to the actualization of others. Hence, which of those things that are possible in principle to human beings are really possible for a particular person depends upon the tradition of actualization in which he or she stands.

There are further aspects of religious doctrine which do not simply emphasize elements of universal experience. The actual history of each Way has introduced doctrines that refer directly to its own practices. For example, there are Buddhist doctrines about the Sangha and about the respective roles of monks and laity, and there are Christian doctrines about the church and the sacraments. These do not appeal to universal self-evidence but to the experiences peculiar to a particular historical movement. There are also teachings about the great figures of the movement and especially about the founder that depend for their warrants on the facts of history as well as on cosmology or metaphysics.

There is a final way in which Christian doctrine has a necessary reference to historical events. In discussing those very few persons who, within a particular province of experience, express completely novel primary intuitions that remain unsurpassed, Whitehead says that "their peculiar originality is the very element in their expression which remains unformularized." (*RM* 130, 131.) This means that the most original element in the life of Jesus will always escape the formula of our systematic doctrines. In Whitehead's words, "Christ gave his life. It is for Christians to discern the doctrine." (*RM* 55.) To do this, it is necessary ever again to return to the "peculiarly vivid record of the first response" (*RM* 55) to this life.

Hence, the reference of Christian faith to historical events, especially the life of Jesus and the first responses to it, is not limited to the fact that these events are responsible for our conscious awareness of particular dimensions of universal prereflective experience. It is also not exhausted by the additional fact that these events have opened up experiences to us which are not experienced prereflectively by all persons. Rather, there is also a continuing dependence upon these events. This continuing reference is based upon faith that there is more in the preformularized accounts of these events than is captured by any set of doctrines about them. Nevertheless, our immediate experience is the final court of appeal. We have faith in the continued fruitfulness of returning to the first accounts of and reactions to Jesus' life for new insights because of the repeated fruitfulness of this return in the past. But this fruitfulness must finally prove itself in our own experience, or faith in the continuing relevance of Jesus will decline in company with other beliefs that do not ring true for us.

The present book is based upon the conviction that a return to Jesus for inspiration is still fruitful. The following chapter offers an interpretation of God that is based in large measure upon a return to the Biblical tradition, and especially the life of Jesus, in contrast with the traditional doctrinal attempts to describe the God to which Jesus witnessed.

3

GOD AS
CREATIVE-RESPONSIVE LOVE

THE EXISTENCE OF GOD

Process theology operates on the one side from the perspective of Christian faith and on the other in the metaphysical context provided by process philosophy and its doctrine of God. Arguments for the existence of God are not an essential part of its work. However, in a day when so many regard belief in God's existence as wholly irrational or view the notion of God as nonsensical, a brief comment on this question is in order.

The word "god" has partly separate histories in religion and in philosophy. In religion the gods are objects of devotion. Their ontological status is not directly in question. In this sense the tribe, the nation-state, or the power of sexuality may be deified. The question of existence arises only when the idea of god becomes conceptually more sophisticated, when religion moves toward philosophy. If that to which devotion is directed is thought to be an inclusive or unifying power, it becomes possible to doubt the existence of "God," for there may be no such unifying power.

The philosopher is interested in some form of ontological primacy or superiority. Thus philosophical doctrines of God vary with the view of reality expressed in the system. One cannot believe in the God of one philosopher if one accepts the conflicting understanding of reality of another philosopher. Viewing the issue of God's existence in these terms, one would question it in general if, with positivists, one regarded all notions of ultimacy as objectionable.

The union of religious and philosophical concerns in classical theism gave the question of the existence of God an apparent definiteness. Much of the modern argument is about the existence of the God of classical theism, especially the God of Thomism. Indeed the word "theism" is often taken in this restricted sense, so that those who affirm the God of the Bible or of Hegel deny that they are theists.

Process thought calls for a freer exploration of the question of God and a looser use of the word "theism." If the word "God" is tightly bound to any particular mode of devotion or view of reality, then in the course of events it will become clear that God does not exist. But this is not a damaging point if "God" is understood more open-endedly, for if "human being" is tightly bound to any particular definition, it eventually becomes apparent that "human beings" do not exist either. But we know that there is an actual referent for "human beings." Likewise, the fact that all conceptualities about God prove inadequate does not show that Jewish, Christian, and Islamic devotion is wholly misplaced or that ontological gradations of primacy are philosophically meaningless. Process thought continues the effort to clarify both the object of theistic worship and the formative ontological elements in reality.

Process philosophy has not produced new arguments for the existence of God. Whitehead found himself compelled to introduce a principle of concretion or limitation to explain the ordered novelty and novel order in the world, but this necessity grew out of his metaphysical analysis of the things of the world. His reasons for affirming God are convincing within the context of his total analysis, but they lose their force if formulated outside his own system of thought.

An example to illustrate the movement of Whitehead's thought to God can be briefly indicated. He envisions a vast congeries of events coming into being momentarily and then lapsing into the past. Each new event must take account of the many events that make up the world given for it. It must do so in some definite way, for without definiteness there is no actuality. Since it has a past different from that of any event in its world, it must have a new form of definiteness. The past cannot impose such a form upon it, since the present can derive from the past only what the past contains. This form of definiteness can be derived only from the sphere of possibility. But the sphere of possibility is purely abstract, lacking all agency to provide selectively for the need of new events. There must be an agency that mediates between these abstract forms or pure possibilities and the actual world. This agency is best conceived as an envisagement of the abstract forms of definiteness such as to establish their graded relevance to every new situation in the actual world. In sum, God is that factor in the universe which establishes what-is-not as relevant to what-is, and lures the world toward new forms of realization.

It has been left to Charles Hartshorne to engage in thorough analysis of the theistic arguments. It is his conviction that the chief weakness of traditional arguments for God has lain in the inadequacy of the idea of God they intended to prove. The ontological argument in particular can be cogently formulated, he believes, but unless the idea of God it seeks to prove is coherent, it serves to disprove rather than to prove it.

The major contribution of process philosophy to the doctrine of God, therefore, is its enrichment and clarification of thought about the divine nature. As a convincing notion of deity emerges that illumines human experience and coheres with our understanding of the world, the demand for an isolated and abstract proof diminishes. A theistic vision of all reality can gain adherence best by displaying its superior adequacy to other visions.

GOD AS RESPONSIVE LOVE

Whitehead noted that whereas in a primitive religion "you study the will of God in order that He may preserve you," in a universal religion "you study his goodness in order to be like him." (*RM* 40.) The Taoist tries to live in harmony with the Tao; the Hindu Vedantist seeks to realize the identity of Atman with Brahman; the Moslem bows to the will of Allah; the Marxist aligns with the dialectical process of history. Accordingly, the statement in Matt.

5:48, "You, therefore, must be perfect, as your heavenly Father is perfect," is a particular expression of the universal religious aspiration of humanity to participate in or be in harmony with perfection. By definition the divine reality is perfect. The question concerns the nature of this perfection.

Christian faith has held that the basic character of this divine reality is best described by the term "love." However, the meaning of the statement "God is love" is by no means self-evident. Whitehead helps us to recover much of the meaning of that phrase as it is found in the New Testament.

We are told by psychologists, and we know from our own experience, that love in the fullest sense involves a sympathetic response to the loved one. Sympathy means feeling the feelings of the other, hurting with the pains of the other, grieving with the grief, rejoicing with the joys. The "others" with whom we sympathize most immediately are the members of our own bodies. When the cells in our hands, for example, are in pain, we share in the pain; we do not view their condition impassively from without. When our bodies are healthy and well exercised, we feel good with them. But we also feel sympathy for other human beings. We would doubt that a husband truly loved his wife if his mood did not to some extent reflect hers.

Nevertheless, traditional theism said that God is completely impassive, that there was no element of sympathy in the divine love for the creatures. The fact that there was an awareness that this Greek notion of divine impassibility was in serious tension with the Biblical notion of divine love for the world is most clearly reflected in this prayer of the eleventh-century theologian Anselm:

Although it is better for thee to be . . . compassionate, passionless, than not to be these things; how art thou . . . compassionate, and, at the same time, passionless? For, if thou art passionless, thou dost not feel sympathy; and if thou dost not feel sympathy, thy heart is not wretched from sympathy for the wretched; but this it is to be compassionate. (Anselm, *Proslogium,* VI and VII, in *Proslogium; Monologium; An Appendix, In Behalf of the Fool, by Gaunilon; and Cur Deus Homo,* tr. by S. N. Deane [The Open Court Publishing Company, 1903, 1945], pp. 11, 13.)

Anselm resolved the tension by saying: "Thou art compassionate in terms of our experience, and not compassionate in terms of thy being." (*Ibid.,* p. 13.) In other words, God only *seems* to us to be compassionate; he is not *really* compassionate! In Anselm's words: "When thou beholdest us in our wretchedness, we experience the effect of compassion, but thou dost not experience the feeling." *(Ibid.)* Thomas Aquinas in the thirteenth century faced the same problem. The objection to the idea that there is love in God was stated as follows: "For in God there are no passions. Now love is a passion. Therefore love is not in God." (*Summa Theologica* I, Q. 20, art. 1, obj. 1.) Thomas responds by making a distinction between two elements within love, one which involves passion and one which does not. He then says, after quoting Aristotle favorably, that God "loves without passion." (*Ibid.,* ans. 1.)

This denial of an element of sympathetic responsiveness to the divine love meant that it was entirely creative. That is, God loves us only in the sense that he does good things for us. In Anselm's words:

> Thou art both compassionate, because thou dost save the wretched, and spare those who sin against thee; and not compassionate, because thou art affected by no sympathy for wretchedness. (*Proslogium,* VII, *loc. cit.,* pp. 13–14.)

In Thomas' words: "To sorrow, therefore, over the misery of others belongs not to God, but it does most properly belong to Him to dispel that misery." (*Summa Theologica* I, Q. 21, art. 3, ans.)

Accordingly, for Anselm and Thomas the analogy is with the father who has no feeling for his children, and hence does not feel their needs, but "loves" them in that he gives good things to them. Thomas explicitly states that "love" is to be understood in this purely outgoing sense, as active goodwill: "To love anything is nothing else than to will good to that thing." He points out that God does not love as we love. For our love is partly responsive, since it is moved by its object, whereas the divine love is purely creative, since it creates its object. (*Summa Theologica* I, Q. 20, art. 2, ans.)

This notion of love as purely creative has implications that are in tension with the Biblical idea of God's equal love for all persons. All persons are obviously not equal in regard to the "good things of life" (however these be defined) that they enjoy (especially in the context of traditional theism, where the majority are consigned to eternal torment). And yet, if God's love is purely creative, totally creating the goodness of the beings loved, this implies that God loves some persons more than others. As Thomas said: "No one thing would be better than another if God did not will greater good for one than for another." (*Summa Theologica* I, Q. 20, art. 3, ans.) This is one of the central ways in which the acceptance of the notion of divine impassibility undercuts the Biblical witness to the love of God.

Since we mold ourselves partly in terms of our image of perfect human existence, and this in turn is based upon our notion of deity, the notion of God as an Impassive Absolute whose love was purely creative could not help but have practical consequences for human existence. Love is often defined by theologians as "active good-will." The notion of sympathetic compassion is missing. Indeed, one of the major theological treatises on the meaning of agape, or Christian love, portrays it as totally outgoing, having no element of responsiveness to the qualities of the loved one. (Anders Nygren, *Agape and Eros* [The Westminster Press, 1953], pp. 77–78.) This notion of love has promoted a "love" that is devoid of genuine sensitivity to the deepest needs of the "loved ones." Is this not why the word "charity," which is derived from *caritas* (the Latin word for agape), today has such heavily negative connotations? Also, the word "do-gooder" is a word of reproach, not because we do not want people to do good things, but because people labeled "do-gooders" go around trying to impose their own notions of the good that needs doing, without any sensitive responsiveness to the real desires and needs of those they think they are helping. This perverted view of love as purely active goodwill is due in large part to the long-standing notion that this is the kind of love which characterizes the divine reality.

This traditional notion of love as solely creative was based upon the value judgment that independence or absoluteness is unqualifiedly good, and that dependence or relativity in any sense derogates from perfection. But, as suggested in Chapter 1, while perfection entails independence or absoluteness in some respects, it also entails dependence or relativity in other respects. It entails ethical independence, in the sense that one should not be deflected by one's passions from the basic commitment to seek the greatest good in all situations. But this ethical commitment, in order to be actualized in concrete situations, requires responsiveness to the actual needs and desires of others. Hence, to promote the greatest good, one must be informed by, and thus relativized by, the feelings of others. Furthermore, we do not admire someone whose enjoyment is not in part dependent upon the condition of those around them. Parents who remained in absolute bliss while their children were in agony would not be perfect—unless there are such things as perfect monsters!

In other words, while there is a type of independence or absoluteness that is admirable, there is also a type of dependence or relativity that is admirable. And, if there is an example of absoluteness that is *unqualifiedly* admirable, this means that there is a divine absoluteness; and the same holds true of relativity. Process thought affirms that both of these are true. While traditional theism spoke only of the divine absoluteness, process theism speaks also of "the divine relativity" (this is the title of one of Hartshorne's books).

Process theism is sometimes called "dipolar theism," in contrast to traditional theism with its doctrine of divine simplicity. For Charles Hartshorne, the two "poles" or aspects of God are the abstract essence of God, on the one hand, and God's concrete actuality on the other. The abstract essence is eternal, absolute, independent, unchangeable. It includes those abstract attributes of deity which characterize the divine existence at every moment. For example, to say that God is omniscient means that in every moment of the divine life God knows everything which is knowable at that time. The concrete actuality is temporal, relative, dependent, and constantly changing. In each moment of God's life there are new, unforeseen happenings in the world which only then have become knowable. Hence, God's concrete knowledge is dependent upon the decisions made by the worldly actualities. God's knowledge is always relativized by, in the sense of internally related to, the world.

Whitehead's way of conceiving the divine dipolarity was not identical with Hartshorne's. Whitehead distinguished between the Primordial Nature of God and the Consequent Nature. The former will be discussed in the following section. The latter is largely identical with what Hartshorne has called God's concrete actuality. Since the Consequent Nature is God as fully actual (*PR* 524, 530), the term "consequent" makes the same point as Hartshorne's term "relative," that God as fully actual is responsive to and receptive of the worldly actualizations.

This divine relativity is not limited to a "bare knowledge" of the new things happening in the world. Rather, the responsiveness includes a sympathetic feeling with the worldly beings, all of whom have feelings. Hence, it is not merely the content of God's knowledge which is dependent, but God's own emotional state. God enjoys our enjoyments, and suffers with our sufferings. This is the kind of responsiveness which is truly divine and belongs to the very nature of perfection. Hence it belongs to the ideal for human existence. Upon this basis, Christian agape can come to have the element of sympathy, of compassion for the present situation of others, which it should have had all along.

GOD AS CREATIVE LOVE

If sympathetic responsiveness is an essential aspect of Christian love, creative activity is no less essential. Whether it be considered a theme or a presupposition, the notion that God is active in the world, working to overcome evil and to create new things, is central to the Biblical tradition. To be in harmony with the God of Israel and of Jesus is to be involved in the struggle to overcome the various impediments to the fullness of life. In Luke 4:18, Jesus quotes from Isaiah, who indicates that the Spirit of the God he worships impels one to "set at liberty those who are oppressed."

The impetus in Western civilization for individual acts and social programs aimed at alleviating human misery and injustice has come in large part from the belief that God not only loves all persons equally, and hence desires justice, but also is directly acting in the world to create just conditions. The reason is that the basic religious drive of humanity is not only to be in harmony with deity, it is also to be in contact with this divine reality. It is because God is personally present and active in the world that contact with the sacred reality does not necessitate fleeing from history. Our activity aimed at creating good puts us in harmony and contact with God. Indeed, this activity can be understood in part as God's acting through us.

Accordingly, the loss of belief in the creative side of God's love would tend to undermine the various liberation movements that have been originally inspired by belief in divine providence, since it is largely this belief which has lent importance to these movements. Cultures in which the sacred is not understood as involved in creating better conditions for life in the world have had difficulty in generating the sustained commitments necessary to bring about significant change.

It is precisely this notion of divine creative activity in the world which has been most problematic in recent centuries, both within theological circles and in the culture at large. In traditional popular Christian thought, God was understood as intervening here and there in the course of the world. The notion of "acts of God" referred to events which did not have natural causes, but were directly caused by God. In traditional theological thought, all events were understood to be totally caused by God, so all events were "acts of God." However, most events were understood to be caused by God through the mediation of worldly or natural causes. God was the "primary cause" of these events, while the natural antecedents were called "secondary causes." However, a few events were thought to be caused directly by God, without the use of secondary causes. These events were "miracles." Accordingly, while all events were in one sense acts of God, these miracles were acts of God in a special sense. Thus, both in popular and theological circles, there was meaning to be given to the idea that God was creatively active in the world.

However, there are two major problems with this notion. First, it raises serious doubt that the creative activity of God can be understood as *love,* since it creates an enormous problem of evil by implying that *every* event in the world is *totally* caused by God, with or without the use of natural causes. Second, since the Renaissance and Enlightenment, the belief has grown that there are no events which happen without natural causes. Accordingly, the notion of "acts of God" has lost all unambiguous referents. Every event termed an act of God was said also, from another perspective, to be totally explainable in terms of natural causation. This rendered the notion of "act of God" of doubtful meaning. If an event can be totally explained in terms of natural forces, i.e., if these provide a "sufficient cause" for it, what justification is there for introducing the idea of "another perspective"? This seems like special pleading in order to retain a vacuous idea.

Deism was a manifestation of the felt difficulty of speaking of divine activity in the world. God's causation was put totally at the beginning of the world process. Once created, the world was said to run autonomously, without any additional divine input. Insofar as some form of this idea has become pervasive in the culture (not to mention complete atheism), the idea that one's activity in the world could put one in harmony and contact with deity has faded.

Twentieth-century theology has reaffirmed the centrality of the idea of God's activity in history. But it has generally lacked the conceptuality for consistently explicating this belief. To a great extent, there has been a return to the idea of the double perspective. Karl Barth had only one complaint regarding the traditional understanding of God's relation to the world: it was not clearly affirmed that the God causing all things is a completely *gracious* God. (*Church Dogmatics* III/3, pp. 31, 118, 146–147.) Formally, Barth said the scheme of primary and secondary causation was correct. (*Ibid.,* pp. 99–100.) Hence, the problem of intelligibility remains. Also, in the light of the tremendous evil unleashed in the twentieth century, the assertion that the God who is in control of the whole process is loving or gracious seems just that—a bare assertion.

Rudolf Bultmann's double perspective presupposes an epistemology in the Kantian tradition. From the objectifying perspective of science and ordinary life, all events are linked together in a chain of cause and effect, which means that "there remains no room for God's working." (*Jesus Christ and Mythology* [Charles Scribner's Sons, 1958], p. 65.) In fact, the essence of myth, and what makes it objectionable, is that it affirms the interruption of the natural course of affairs by attributing a natural effect to a supernatural cause. (*Kerygma and Myth*, ed. by Hans Werner Bartsch, tr. by Reginald H. Fuller [London: SPCK, 1953], p. 197.) But from the perspective of faith, the believer can in the moment confess that an event is "nevertheless" an act of God. *(Ibid.)* The believer affirms a paradoxical identity between a divine act and a fully natural event. The problem of evil is raised less clearly by Bultmann's position, but the problem of intelligibility remains, at least for all those who cannot accept an irreducibly dual perspective.

Bonhoeffer's negation of the "God of the gaps" is a protest against the idea of God as intervening here and there in the world, especially to solve human problems. In this respect Bonhoeffer makes the same negative point as Bultmann. But Bonhoeffer (in the brief period he had as a theologian) provided no positive alternative way of understanding the divine creative presence in the world, beyond the suggestion that we view it as in the midst rather than at the periphery of life. Paul Tillich's theology, in which God is "being-itself" and not "a being" interacting with others, involves a denial that God is a causal influence in the world, even though much of Tillich's language illegitimately gives the impression that creative influence is being exerted by God.

In Western culture generally, the problem of evil, and the widespread belief that the nexus of natural cause and effect excludes divine "intervention," have combined to render the notion of divine creative love problematic. When the leading secular thinkers then see that the leading theologians have provided no intelligible means for speaking of God's activity in the world, they are confirmed in their suspicion that this belief belongs to the myths of the past. Process theology provides a way of recovering the conviction that God acts creatively in the world and of understanding this creative activity as the expression of divine *love* for the world. The notion that there is a creative power of love behind and within the worldly process is no longer one which can only be confessed in spite of all appearances to the contrary. Instead it illuminates our experience.

DIVINE CREATIVE LOVE
AS PERSUASIVE

As indicated in the Foreword, traditional theism portrayed God as the Controlling Power. The doctrine of divine omnipotence finally meant that God controlled every detail of the world process. Some traditional theologians, such as Thomas Aquinas, muted this implication of their thought as much as possible (in order to protect the doctrine of human freedom). Others, such as Luther and Calvin, proclaimed the doctrine from the housetops (in order to guard against both pride and anxiety). But, in either case, the doctrine followed logically from other doctrines that were affirmed. The notion that God knows the world, and that this knowledge is unchanging, suggests that God must in fact determine every detail of the world, lest something happen which was not immutably known. The doctrine that God is completely independent of the world implies that the divine knowledge of it cannot be dependent upon it, and this can only be if the world does nothing which was not totally determined by God. The doctrine of divine simplicity involves the assertion that all the divine attributes are identical; hence God's knowing the world is identical with God's causing it. The Biblical record is quite ambivalent on the question of whether God is in complete control of the world. There is much in the Bible which implies that divine providence is not all-determining. But the interpretation of the Biblical God in terms of valuations about perfection derived from Greek philosophy ruled out this side of the Biblical witness, thereby making creaturely freedom vis-à-vis God merely apparent.

Process thought, with its different understanding of perfection, sees the divine creative activity as based upon responsiveness to the world. Since the very meaning of actuality involves internal relatedness, God as an actuality is essentially related to the world. Since actuality as such is partially self-creative, future events are not yet determinate, so that even perfect knowledge cannot know the future, and God does not wholly control the world. Any divine creative influence must be persuasive, not coercive.

Whitehead's fundamentally new conception of divine creativity in the world centers around the notion that God provides each worldly actuality with an "initial aim." This is an impulse, initially felt conformally by the occasion, to actualize the best possibility open to it, given its concrete situation. But this initial aim does not automatically become the subject's own aim. Rather, this "subjective aim" is a product of its own decision. The subject may choose to actualize the initial aim; but it may also choose from among the other real possibilities open to it, given its context. In other words, God seeks to persuade each occasion toward that possibility for its own existence which would be best for it; but God cannot control the finite occasion's self-actualization. Accordingly, the divine creative activity involves risk. The obvious point is that, since God is not in complete control of the events of the world, the occurrence of genuine evil is not incompatible with God's beneficence toward all his creatures.

A less obvious but equally important consequence is that, since persuasion and not control is the divine way of doing things, this is the way we should seek to accomplish our ends. Much of the tragedy in the course of human affairs can be attributed to the feeling that to control others, and the course of events, is to share in divinity. Although traditional theism said that God was essentially love, the divine love was subordinated to the divine power. Although the result of Jesus' message, life, and death should have been to redefine divine power in terms of the divine love, this did not happen. Power, in the sense of controlling domination, remained the *essential* definition of deity. Accordingly, the control of things, events, and other persons, which is to some extent a "natural" human tendency, took on that added sense of satisfaction which comes from participating in an attribute understood (more or less consciously) to be divine.

Process theology's understanding of divine love is in harmony with the insight, which we can gain both from psychologists and from our own experience, that if we truly love others we do not seek to control them. We do not seek to pressure them with promises and threats involving extrinsic rewards and punishments. Instead we try to persuade them to actualize those possibilities which they themselves will find intrinsically rewarding. We do this by providing ourselves as an environment that helps open up new, intrinsically attractive possibilities.

Insofar as the notion that divine love is persuasive is accepted, the exercise of persuasive influence becomes intrinsically rewarding. It takes on that aura of extra importance that has too often been associated with the feeling of controlling others. This change has implications in all our relations, from one-to-one I-thou encounters to international relations. It does not mean that coercive control could be eliminated, but it does mean that such control is exercised as a last resort and with a sense of regret rather than with the thrill that comes from the sense of imitating deity.

DIVINE CREATIVE LOVE
AS PROMOTING ENJOYMENT

In traditional Christianity, God has been understood as a Cosmic Moralist, in the sense of being *primarily* concerned with the development of moral behavior and attitudes in human beings. Negatively, this meant that the promotion of creaturely enjoyment was not God's first concern. In fact, in most Christian circles enjoyment has been understood as something that God at best tolerated, and often as something that he opposed. Thus the pleasure of sexual relations is tolerated, as long as it is only a concomitant of the primary function of sex, which is the morally sound intention to have children. The use of contraceptives has been frowned upon, since their use would mean the explicit admission that sexual intercourse was being engaged in solely for the enjoyment it brings.

This attitude toward sex is only the extreme example of the church's traditional attitude toward enjoyment in general, which has been taken to be a reflection of God's attitude. The result has been a stern, lifeless Christianity, being in tension with rather than supportive of the natural drive to enjoy life. The man whom Christians have called the Christ was called by some a "glutton and a drunkard" (Matt. 11:19; Luke 7:34) and could be quoted by one of the Evangelists as saying, "I came that they may have life, and have it abundantly" (John 10:10). But the Christian church has been perceived, not as the community that encourages the enjoyment of the abundant life, but as the institution that discourages most forms of enjoyment in the name of "being good." To put it crudely, one does not attend church to have a good time, but to atone for the good time one had the night before! God has been understood as commanding us to suppress our desire for most of those experiences which we find *intrinsically* good in favor of being *morally* good. And moral goodness has primarily been understood negatively, that is, as involving the suppression of many of the natural forms of enjoyment.

This notion of God as Cosmic Moralist is not unrelated to the idea of God as Controlling Power. The problem of evil would too evidently disprove the existence of God, if God be understood not only as controlling all events but also as willing the maximum enjoyment of his creatures. If the primary focus is on the creatures' enjoyment of existence, the great amount and variety of suffering and the great inequalities involved would easily suggest that God was either malevolent or incompetent, if not both. Hence, the notion that God is competently in control of all things can be saved by saying that creaturely enjoyment is not a high priority. In fact, the sufferings of life, and even the inequalities in this regard, can be regarded as divinely intended means to promote the desired moral and religious attitudes.

Hence, the notion of God as Cosmic Moralist supports the notion of God as Controlling Power. A development in this regard in the history of Christian thought can be detected. In the earlier centuries, and especially in the thought of Augustine, there was a heavy stress on the intrinsic goodness of being actual. This stress was supported by the goodness of the creation as declared by God in Gen., ch. 1, and the Platonic equation of being and goodness. This position was maintained throughout the Middle Ages—it is still dominant in Thomas Aquinas, for example—in spite of the added difficulty it creates for the problem of evil. This was possible partly because the Biblical and rational proofs for the existence of

God (as conceived by traditional theists) were thought to be so strong that the problem of evil could be dismissed. However, in modern times, especially in Protestant thought, the idea of the intrinsic goodness of existence has faded, and Christian theology has become increasingly moralistic. This is no doubt due to several factors. The ontological dualism of the modern age, especially in its Cartesian variety, made it difficult to think of existence as such as intrinsically good, since humans were the only created beings with any intrinsic (experiential) reality. Also, the loss of confidence in the rational and then the Biblical evidences for God's existence made the problem of evil more desperate. Accordingly, and especially in modern Protestant thought, the dominant trend in theodicy has been to explain the great sufferings of the world by declaring that God did not intend the world as a "hedonistic paradise," but as a "vale of soul-making." (Cf. John Hick, *Evil and the God of Love* [Harper & Row, Publishers, Inc., 1966], pp. 291–297; and A. C. Knudson, *The Doctrine of Redemption* [Abingdon Press, 1933], p. 215.)

Process theology sees God's fundamental aim to be the promotion of the creatures' own enjoyment. God's creative influence upon them is loving, because it aims at promoting that which the creatures experience as intrinsically good. Since God is not in complete control, the divine love is not contradicted by the great amount of intrinsic evil, or "disenjoyment," in the world. The creatures in part create both themselves and their successors.

God's creative love extends to all the creatures, since all actualities, as experiential, have some degree of enjoyment. The promotion of enjoyment is God's primary concern throughout the whole process of creative evolution. The contrary doctrine, which sees God's primary concern to be the development of moral attitudes, is in the uncomfortable position of maintaining that over 99 percent of the history of our planet was spent in merely preparing the way for beings who are capable of the only kind of experience that really interests God.

Enjoyment is God's primary concern even with those beings who are capable of developing moral attitudes. But this is not in conflict with an emphasis on morality. God wants us to enjoy, true.

But he wants us *all* to enjoy. Accordingly, he wants us to enjoy in ways that do not unnecessarily inhibit enjoyment on the part of others. That puts it negatively. Positively stated, God wants our enjoyment to be such as to increase the enjoyments of others. To be moral is to actualize oneself in such a way as to maximize the enjoyments of future actualities, insofar as these future enjoyments can be conditioned by one's present decision. Hence, although the development of moral attitudes is of extreme importance, it is a derivative concern, secondary to the primary value, which is enjoyment itself.

In traditional Christianity, morality and enjoyment were often seen as in fundamental opposition. In process thought, morality stands in the service of enjoyment. However, the question still arises of the possible tension between them. There is the possible tension between enjoying the present moment to the hilt, and forgoing some of this possible enjoyment in order to prepare for increased enjoyment in the future. Also there is the tension, in regard to the future, between my *own* future occasions of experience, and the future experiences of other enduring individuals. This tension, and its ideal resolution, will be discussed in Chapter 5. Suffice it here to say that the creative love of God is also relevant to this problem. The divine initial aim for our human experiences is such as to transform into immediate enjoyment the intention to contribute to future good.

DIVINE CREATIVE LOVE
AS ADVENTUROUS

One respect in which God's creative love is adventurous has already been discussed: since God's creative activity is persuasive, not controlling, it is a love that takes risks. Hence, each divine creative impulse into the world is adventurous, in that God does not know what the result will be.

However, there is another dimension to the divine adventurousness. Traditional theology tended to portray God as the Sanctioner of the Status Quo. The notions of "God" and "order" were closely associated. In the political realm, the connection between obedience to God and submission to the political status quo was supported by the notorious appeal to Rom., ch. 13, where Paul says that we should "be subject to the governing authorities" because they "have been instituted by God," so that "he who resists the authorities resists what God has appointed."

This notion of God is also closely connected with the notion of God as Controlling Power. Paul's statement is one of those Biblical statements which presuppose that God is in control at least of the major features of the world process. The development of traditional theism, in which God was more consistently said to be in complete control of every detail, further strengthened the conviction that the political status quo should be affirmed. For if God had not wanted those rulers in power, they would not be in power. It is largely due to this notion that those who have been in opposition to despotic rulers have also found themselves in opposition to the church, and have found it useful to espouse atheism.

In the realm of morality in general, belief in God has been closely associated with the idea of moral absolutes, especially of a negative nature. Certain kinds of actions have been said to be wrong in themselves, whether or not in a particular context they served to promote abundant life. This has focused moral attention on rules or fixed principles and distracted from consideration of what would increase the quality of life in the future. Hence the notion that Christian morality consists primarily in abstaining from certain kinds of acts that God has prohibited serves doubly to sanction the status quo. It does so directly, simply by virtue of the notion of immutable moral absolutes. It does so indirectly by diverting attention from the primary moral question of how we should act so as to increase enjoyment of life now and in the future.

The notion of God as Sanctioner of the Status Quo is closely connected with that of God as Cosmic Moralist. The focus on the development of moral attitudes, understood as being in opposition to the growth of enjoyment, distracted attention from the question of what kinds of conditions are needed in order to maximize the possibilities for enjoying existence. This question was not of ultimate importance, since moral attitudes can be developed in any situation. In fact, as some theologians have argued, the more difficult the circumstances, the greater the opportunity for developing moral qualities such as patience!

Process theology understands God precisely as the basic source of unrest in the universe. In Whitehead's words, "The pure conservative is fighting against the essence of the universe." (*AI* 354.) When he speaks of the essence of the universe, Whitehead primarily has in mind the notion that actuality is process, and that at the root of process there is the Primordial Nature of God, which he sometimes calls the Divine Eros. This is conceived as "the active entertainment of all ideals, with the urge to their finite realization, each in its due season." (*AI* 357.) Not all ideal possibilities can be realized simultaneously. This is why there is process. (*MT* 53.) But also no ideal can be repeated indefinitely without its freshness being lost. The Primordial Nature of God is the goad toward novelty in the universe (*PR* 135), stimulating us to realize new possibilities after the old ones no longer are sufficient to give zest to our enjoyment of being actual.

Order is an essential ingredient in the maximization of enjoyment. For example, the richness of human experience could emerge only on the basis of the order of the body. "It is by reason of the body, with its miracle of order, that the treasures of the past environment are poured into the living occasion." (*PR* 516.) On the other hand, excessive order can inhibit enjoyment. Hence, Whitehead speaks of "the contrast between order as the condition for excellence, and order as stifling the freshness of living." (*PR* 514.) Hence, order must not be lost, but it also must not be dominant. "The art of progress is to preserve order amid change, and to preserve change amid order." (*PR* 515.)

God is the source of order. But two important qualifications must be made. Order represents dominance of an ideal possibility which was at one time a novel element in the world. Hence God is the source of order by virtue of first being the source of novelty. Second, neither order nor novelty is understood as intrinsically good, but only as instrumental to the one intrinsic good, which is the enjoyment of intense experience. "God's purpose in the creative advance is the evocation of intensities. The evocation of societies is purely subsidiary to this absolute end." (*PR* 161.) " 'Order' and 'novelty' are but the instruments of his subjective aim which is the intensification of 'formal immediacy.' " (*PR* 135.) In brief, although God is the source of order, the order is derivative from novelty, and both order and novelty are good only insofar as they contribute to the enjoyment of experience. As Whitehead puts it elsewhere, the aim toward order, which is impersonal, is subservient to the love of individuals, which is personal. Therefore, types of order are to be rated "according to their success in magnifying the individual actualities, that is to say, in promoting strength of experience." (*AI* 376.)

Hence, no type of social order is to be maintained if it no longer tends to maximize the enjoyment of the members of the society. Also, it is impossible for any form of social order to continue indefinitely to be instrumentally good. God, far from being the Sanctioner of the Status Quo, is the source of some of the chaos in the world. "If there is to be progress beyond limited ideals, the course of history by way of escape must venture along the borders of chaos in its substitution of higher for lower types of order." (*PR* 169.) (God is said to be the source of only *some* of the chaos, since only some of it can in principle lead to a higher type of order and thereby a richer form of enjoyment.)

The connection between the notion of God as the source of adventure toward novel ideals and that of divine creative love as fostering enjoyment has already been made clear. The connection with God as persuasive power is also obvious. Since God does not control the details of any worldly process, the existence of a given state of affairs does not imply that God willed it. Further, since God encourages the actualization of novel possibilities as a means to maximizing creaturely enjoyment, continuation of a state of affairs that originally resulted from a high degree of conformity to God's aims may not express God's present will. As Henry Nelson Wieman has stressed, partly under the influence of Whitehead, we should worship the Creative Good, not the created good.

Besides the two senses already mentioned in which God's love is adventurous—that it takes risks and promotes adventure toward novelty in the world—there is a third sense. This results from combining this creative side of God's love (God as Divine Eros) with the responsive side. The result is, in Whitehead's words, "the concept of an Adventure in the Universe as One." (*AI* 380.) This is simply a way of describing God. "This Adventure embraces all particular occasions but as an actual fact stands beyond any one of them." (*Ibid.*) The point is that God's own life is an adventure, for the novel enjoyments that are promoted among the creatures are then the experiences providing the material for God's own enjoyment. "The Unity of Adventure includes the Eros which is the living urge towards all possibilities, claiming the goodness of their realization." (*AI* 381.) And God's life is also an adventure in the sense of being a risk, since God will feel the discord as well as the beautiful experiences involved in the finite actualizations: "The Adventure of the Universe starts with the dream and reaps tragic Beauty." (*Ibid.*)

GOD AS CREATIVE-
RESPONSIVE LOVE

The traditional concept of God is in many respects stereotypically masculine. God was conceived to be active, unresponsive, impassive, inflexible, impatient, and moralistic. This being had none of the stereotypically feminine traits—it was not at all passive, responsive, emotional, flexible, patient, and it did not balance moral concern with an appreciation of beauty. This has led to a one-sided and hence unhealthy Christianity.

An overreaction resulting in a concept of God devoid of the stereotypically masculine attributes would also be destructive of authentic Christian existence. Losing the active or creative side of the divine love would undercut much of the good that Biblical faiths have brought into history, as we have already suggested. The same is true of the strong element of moral concern that has been attributed to God in the cultures decisively influenced by the Biblical faiths. Likewise, the loss of the notion of a divine purpose that at its most general level is inflexible would lead to a complete relativism. The positive aspects of these "masculine" attributes can be retained, without their destructive implications, if they are incorporated into a revolutionized concept of God into which the stereotypically feminine traits are integrated. For, in the integrated result, the former traits are changed qualitatively.

Unfortunately, in some passages Whitehead does not describe the two "natures" of God as if they were truly integrated. Sometimes the Primordial Nature is described as if it were static order of the eternal possibilities, and the "initial aim" for each worldly actuality is said to be derived from this Primordial Nature. This would mean that the creative input of God into the world in each moment would be based upon a completely inflexible vision; it would not be based upon a sympathetic response to the previous state of affairs. However, in other passages Whitehead makes it clear that the ideals toward which the world is called by God in one moment are based upon God's loving response to the facts of the previous moments. (*RM* 148–149, 151, 152.) The world does not really have to do with two "natures" or "poles" of God that stand externally related to each other, the one influencing the world and the other being influenced by it. Rather, the Primordial Nature is abstract, while the Consequent Nature is God as fully actual. (*PR* 524, 532.) It is finally to God as a whole that we are related. The creative activity of God is based upon sympathetic responsiveness; and the responsiveness of God is an active receptiveness made in the light of an intended creative influence upon the future.

The process dipolar notion of deity has some affinity with the Taoist notion of the Tao, in which the "feminine" and "masculine" (yin and yang) dimensions of reality are perfectly integrated. The Tao is spoken of as a power that works slowly and undramatically, but is finally the most effective agency in reality. Whereas there are aspects of the notion of the Tao which have unfortunate implications, the Taoist vision of deity does contain an important element which should all along have been part of the Christian vision.

4

A THEOLOGY OF NATURE

The present chapter sketches in broad strokes three aspects of a theology of nature. The first section presents an interpretation of the evolutionary development of the world as rooted in the divine creative activity. The second section explains how process theology deals with the problem of theodicy. And the third section, building on what has been said in Chapter 1, supports an ecological attitude.

WHY AN EVOLUTIONARY PROCESS?

Traditional theism had trouble explaining why there should be a world. The description of deity as *actus purus* meant that God had already (i.e., eternally) actualized all possible values. This was one way of stressing deity's total independence of the world. Process theology does not have this problem. Although the possible values all subsist in God, they subsist as merely *possible* values, not as actualized values. They are possible values for finite realization. They are in God only conceptually, or in the mode of appetition, not physically, or in the mode of enjoyment. Hence, there must be a world of finite actualities, or no values will be enjoyed.

However, since all actualities have value, the question still remains as to why these actualities should be involved in an evolutionary process. The basic element of the answer to this question is that there are gradations of value, and some actualities are capable of greater enjoyment than others. Roughly speaking, more complex actualities enjoy more value than simpler ones. The direction of the evolutionary process on the whole is toward more complex actualities, resulting from God's basic creative purpose, which is the evocation of actualities with greater and greater enjoyment.

If traditional theists gave up the idea of God as *actus purus,* but held to the notion of God as Controlling Power, they would still have difficulty explaining why there has been an evolutionary process. The difficulty is increased when it is anthropocentrically assumed, as it usually is, that the last (or at least latest) act of the drama of creation, the human species, is the only one with any real value, and that the rest was mere prologue. But it is still difficult on the more modest assumption, which we all in practice hold, that the more complex developments have more value than the earlier, simpler ones, since nothing has any inherent power to resist the divine Controlling Power. Whatever God wills can be brought about immediately. Why, then, take over four billion years to get to the more valuable creatures, if they could have been created at once?

This problem also does not exist for process theology, since it rejects the idea of God as Controlling Power. In Whitehead's approving description of Plato's thought, God's influence "is always persuasive, and can only produce such order as is possible." (*AI* 189.) Another crucial assumption is that the more complex forms of order presuppose the simpler forms, and hence can only come after them. In the remainder of this section we will provide a sketch, based upon Whitehead's suggestions, of the major steps in this evolution of more complex forms of order.

But first the reason for the positive correlation between complexity and enjoyment must be made explicit. The two variables involved in the degree of enjoyment are harmony and intensity. Obviously, for experience to be enjoyable, it must be basically harmonious; the elements must not clash so strongly that discord outweighs harmony. Also, for great enjoyment there must be adequate intensity of experience. Without intensity there might be harmony, but the value enjoyed will be trivial. Intensity depends upon complexity, since intensity requires that a variety of elements be brought together into a unity of experience. To bring a variety of elements into a moment of experience means to *feel* these elements, to prehend them *positively*. Now, the more complex an actuality is, the more elements from its environment it can feel, and thereby take into itself. The simpler occasions of experience must exclude from feeling more of the potential values in the environment. This is why intensity depends upon complexity, and hence why the higher grades of enjoyment finally depend upon complexity. Furthermore, a complex actuality is possible only on the basis of an ordered environment. This is why order is promoted for the sake of increased enjoyment.

These criteria of harmony and intensity (based on variety held in contrast) are taken from aesthetics. Whitehead accordingly uses the word "beauty" to describe the achievement of an occasion of experience that fulfills these criteria. To maximize beauty is to maximize enjoyment. God's purpose, then, can be described as the aim toward maximizing either beauty or enjoyment. It is on the basis of these criteria of intrinsic value that the evolutionary process can be viewed as in part a product of divine providence.

Process theology rejects the notion of *creatio ex nihilo,* if that means creation out of *absolute* nothingness. That doctrine is part and parcel of the doctrine of God as absolute controller. Process theology affirms instead a doctrine of creation out of chaos (which was suggested not only by Plato but also by more Old Testament passages than those supporting the doctrine of creation out of nothing). A state of absolute chaos would be one in which there is nothing but very low-grade actual occasions happening at random, i.e., without being ordered into enduring individuals. An enduring individual is a series of occasions, each of which inherits more significantly from the preceding occasion in that series than it does from the other actualities in its environment. Electrons and protons are examples. By transmitting identical characteristics from occasion to occasion they maintain individual identity through long periods of time. In a chaotic situation, on the contrary, each occasion would inherit equally from all the previous contiguous actualities. Whitehead suggests that what we refer to as the "empty space" between astronomical bodies is really full of chaotic occasions; it is only "empty" of any enduring individuals. (*PR* 141, 142; *SMW* 122, 220–221.)

There is value even when the situation is chaotic, since there are still actual occasions and all occasions have some intrinsic value. But the value enjoyed must be extremely trivial. With no order among the occasions, their respective contributions cannot be combined; the data provided for the enjoyment of a burgeoning subject are the outcome of mutually thwarting decisions. (*PR* 142.) This provides one sense in which the present world can be said to be the result of creation out of nothing. The chaos from which it emerged was a "nothingness of confusion." (*Imm.* 691.) We normally have an enduring individual in mind when we speak of a "thing"; in this sense the primordial chaos contained no-*thing*.

The first stage of creation of order out of this chaos, then, was the development of things, or enduring individuals. In Whitehead's words: "There must have been some epoch in which the dominant trend was the formation of protons, electrons, molecules. . . ." (*FR* 24.) Now, these simple enduring individuals involve the repetition of some particular form. This repetition in itself adds intensity to the actualization of the value in question. (*SMW* 137, 152–153, 278; *Imm.* 688–690.) This is the most primitive example of the fact that order is a condition for intensity of experience. (*MT* 87; *PR* 373 f.) This development of primitive enduring individuals is the first stage in the escape from triviality.

However, besides increasing the enjoyment in the world, this degree of order provides the necessary basis for a higher degree of order to appear, which would allow for even greater enjoyment. This illustrates the connection between novelty and order. There is evidently an order among the possibilities themselves. They cannot be actualized in the world in simply any order; rather, some become *real* possibilities only after others have been actualized. Hence, at one stage certain novel possibilities are actualized for the first time. If they are then repeated, they become part of the order of the world. As such they provide the conditions for other novel possibilities to become actualized. And so on.

The development of enduring individuals at the level of electrons, protons, neutrons, etc., provided the necessary condition for the emergence of atoms. The atoms in turn provided the necessary condition for the appearance of molecules. These in turn were necessary ingredients in the emergence of the living cell.

Each stage of the evolutionary process represents an increase in the divinely given possibilities for value that are actualized. The present builds upon the past but advances beyond the past to the degree to which it responds to the divine impulses. This advance is experienced as intrinsically good, and it also provides the condition for an even richer enjoyment of existence in the future.

The increase of intrinsic value in the advance from chaos to events at the electronic-protonic level, and on to the atomic and molecular levels, is real but trivial. The increase is primarily in instrumental value. Atoms and molecules fit Whitehead's description of actualities "which, trivial in their own proper character of immediate 'ends,' are proper 'means' for the emergence of a world . . . intrinsically of immediate worth." (*PR* 517.)

The living cell is evidently another story. It is not ontologically different from the actualities that came before it. (The discovery of levels of actuality in between cells and "ordinary" molecules has further supported this Whiteheadian view.) However, it is significantly different. In Whitehead's words:

> In a sense, the difference between a living organism and the inorganic environment is only a question of degree; but it is a difference of degree which makes all the difference—in effect, it is a difference of quality. (*PR* 271.)

The word "living" points to the difference. All occasions of experience have at least the germ of mentality, for "mentality" is simply the capacity for self-determination: "The mental pole introduces the subject as a determinant of its own concrescence." (*PR* 380.) But in nonliving occasions, the mentality is "merely the appetition towards, or from, whatever in fact already is." (*FR* 33.) Although it is the element of final causation in the actualities, "it is degraded to being merely one of the actors in the efficient causation." (*FR* 34.) In other words, it brings nothing new into the world, but simply repeats the past, or lets it decay.

A "living" actuality is one in which the mental pole introduces a novel element into itself, one which was not derived from the past world. (*PR* 156, 159.) This increases the value that can be enjoyed. The fact that a novel element is introduced by itself increases the variety and hence the intensity of the experience. And the novel response to the environment is a way of converting otherwise incompatible elements into compatible contrasts that can be internally appropriated. This further increases the intensity of enjoyment.

Accordingly, God's success as the goad toward novelty increases the present enjoyment in the world by stimulating the emergence of life. However, as before, this advance in intrinsic value has its instrumental value for the future. Cells can be so organized that a yet higher series of experiences can emerge from them. The reference here, of course, is to animals, especially those with a central nervous system. The higher stream of experience is the animal soul. (The notion of the psyche or soul is explained in Chapter 5.)

Each stage of this process of complexification (to use Teilhard's term), which increases the capacity for enjoyment, presupposes the previous stage. Each novel advance was possible only after the previous novel advance had become stabilized into a pervasive order. Also, only a limited advance is possible at each stage—it is not possible to jump directly from stage one to stage four; stages two and three have to come in between. Cells could not emerge directly out of electrons and protons, for the experiences they enjoy, and hence the data they have to contribute to others, are too trivial. Likewise, a soul as complex as that of a squirrel could not emerge directly out of molecules.

On the basis of this correlation between novelty and increasingly complex order, on the one hand, and increased capacity for enjoyment, on the other, the evolutionary development of our world propounded by modern science can be interpreted in harmony with the character and purpose of God. This creatively and responsively loving God is incarnately active in the present, bringing about immediate good on the basis of activity in the past, and with the purpose to bring about greater good in the future—a greater good that will involve a fuller incarnation of the divine reality itself.

Why So Much Evil
in the World?

If God is perfect in power and loving goodness, why is there so much evil in the world? In fact, why is there *any* evil at all? Traditional theism answered this question by finally denying that there is any evil in the world. They said that all *apparent* evil was really, from the ultimate perspective, a means to good, and hence was not *genuinely* evil. Even though they had to admit that God, as the Controlling Power, was *responsible* for every detail of the world, and hence for all (apparent) evil, they could say that God was not *indictable,* since "all things work together for good." Traditional theists from Augustine to Aquinas, Calvin, and Schleiermacher have essentially agreed with the eighteenth-century words of Alexander Pope:

> All discord, harmony not understood;
> All partial evil, universal good;
> And, spite of pride, in erring reason's spite,
> One truth is clear, Whatever is, is right.

Process theology also says that God is responsible for evil but not indictable for it. But unlike traditional theism it does not deny that there is genuine evil. On the contrary, there are events that would have been better otherwise, all things considered. In place of some events that have occurred, other possible events could have occurred then and there that would have been better. This is one of those universal convictions to which any philosophy or theology must be adequate if it is to be acceptable.

Process theology distinguishes between divine responsibility and blameworthiness on the basis of three central notions. The first has already been clarified—the power of God is persuasive, not controlling. Finite actualities can fail to conform to the divine aims for them. "So far as the conformity is incomplete, there is evil in the world." (*RM* 60.) This deviation is not necessary; hence evil is not necessary. But the possibility for the deviation is necessary; hence the possibility of evil is necessary.

But why is the possibility for so much evil necessary? The second notion is that there are two kinds of experience that are equally evil, and hence to be avoided: triviality and discord. But there is a distinction to be made. Discord, which is physical or mental suffering, is simply evil in itself, whenever it occurs. (*AI* 329–330, 342.) Triviality, however, is only evil in some cases. A trivial enjoyment is not evil in itself; in fact, as an enjoyment, it is intrinsically good, insofar as its harmony outweighs its discordant elements. But if it is more trivial and hence less intense than it could have been, given the real possibilities open to it, then it is evil. (*RM* 94.) Hence, while discord is absolutely evil, triviality is only comparatively evil. The two forms of nonmoral evil, then, are discord and *unnecessary* triviality.

These two forms of evil are simply the two characteristics that can prevent the maximization of enjoyment, which is the one intrinsic good. A morally good being, positively stated, is simply one who seeks to maximize that which is intrinsically good. This means, negatively, that a morally good being would seek to prevent both discord and unnecessary triviality.

However, in most considerations of the problem of evil, nonmoral evil is equated with physical and mental suffering, i.e., discord, with the result that unnecessary triviality is ignored. Accordingly, the discussion proceeds as if God's only concern should be to minimize or eliminate all discord. But if this were the sole criterion of moral perfection, then—proceeding to the logical conclusion—God would have abstained from creating a world altogether, that being the only way to guarantee the absence of all suffering! Within the context of process thought, this would mean that God would not stimulate the chaos to incarnate increasingly complex forms of order. There is probably some discord even in empty space, of course, but it must be extremely trivial. Hence, if the sole concern were with avoiding as much suffering as possible, an everlasting chaos would be the solution.

But, even though we sometimes speak as if this is what moral goodness is all about, we really know better. We know that it should primarily be positively rather than negatively defined. The morally admirable being is one who promotes worthwhile experience to the quantitatively and qualitatively greatest possible extent.

Accordingly, God's loving purpose must not be thought of as merely the avoidance of discord. To have left the finite realm in chaos, when it could have been stimulated to become a world, would have been to acquiesce in unnecessary triviality. To be loving or moral, God's aim must be to overcome unnecessary triviality while avoiding as much discord as possible. In other words, the aim is for the perfection of experience. Perfection is the maximal harmonious intensity that is possible for a creature, given its context. The more variety and hence intensity there is, the greater the possibilities for disharmony. But this is a necessary risk, if there is to be a chance for the perfection of experience to be attained. In Whitehead's words, the evil of discord "is the half-way house between perfection and triviality." (*AI* 355.)

Clarifying this point requires the third major notion relevant to explaining why the possibility of so much evil is necessary. This notion is that there is a correlation among the following dimensions of experience: (1) the capacity for intrinsic good; (2) the capacity for intrinsic evil; (3) the capacity for instrumental good; (4) the capacity for instrumental evil; (5) the power for self-determination. The correlation among these dimensions of experience is positive, meaning that if any one of them increases, the others also proportionally increase.

Further, the correlation is necessary rather than contingent. It is not dependent upon a choice, even a divine choice. Traditional theism denied that there are any necessary because uncreated principles governing the interrelations among worldly actualities, and hence God's relations with them, other than strictly logical principles. This rejection of uncreated and hence necessary principles fits with the doctrine that the existence of finite actualities is strictly contingent, and that they were created out of absolute nothingness. If it is not necessary that there be finite actualities, and if in fact they have not always existed, it makes no sense to talk about necessary principles governing their mutual relations and therefore limiting what God can do with them. But if there has always been a realm of finite actualities, and if the existence of such a realm (though not with any particular order) is as eternal and necessary as is the existence of God, then it also makes sense to think of eternally necessary principles descriptive of their possible relationships.

Accordingly, if God is to bring an ordered world out of a chaos of finite actualities, any development that God can promote will have to conform to these correlations. The positive correlation between the capacity for intrinsic good and intrinsic evil means, as already indicated, that the increased complexity that makes greater enjoyment possible also makes greater suffering possible. Greater complexity of experience overcomes triviality, but it does not guarantee bliss, for it may open the door to discord so great that the positive enjoyment of experience will be virtually eliminated. The reason is that the condition for great enjoyment is the capacity to receive the feelings of others into oneself. This is good if the feelings the others contribute are by and large harmonious. But if they are not—if one's body is wracked with pain, if loved ones are mutilated—then the sympathetic appropriation of their feelings becomes the source of great suffering. In fact, the suffering can be so great that sympathetic appropriation can seem more a curse than a blessing, and practices can be undertaken to seek to eliminate or at least minimize this capacity. One can choose harmony over intensity, thus reverting to a more trivial existence in order to avert discord.

On the happier side, there is a correlation between intrinsic good and instrumental good. This correlation has been implicit in our description of the stages of the evolutionary process. Each stage in the process of complexification meant an increase in the capacity for present value, or enjoyment; but it was also a necessary condition for a further stage. These richer individuals have more to contribute to others. Only actualities with the intensity enjoyed by living cells could provide the context out of which souls could emerge. Likewise, human beings have values to contribute to others which the lower animals do not have—most people do not find the company of pets sufficient.

At the same time, the capacity for instrumental good correlates with the capacity for instrumental evil. Whereas our bodily cells can be the source of some of our greatest enjoyments, as in the enjoyment of food, drink, exercise, and sex, they can also be the source of some of our greatest sufferings, as when they are deprived of their needs, or when their environment is forcing elements into them which they cannot harmonize. Some of the feelings that cannot be harmonized may have come from the previous experiences of the soul itself, as in psychosomatic illness.

On the basis of the positive correlations among these first four dimensions of experience, we see that the development of beings with the capacity to enjoy significant values, and to contribute significant values to those beyond themselves, necessarily meant the development of beings with the capacity to undergo significant suffering, and to contribute significantly to the suffering of others beyond themselves. The good cannot be had without the possibility of the bad. To escape triviality necessarily means to risk discord.

Correlative with these four dimensions is the capacity for self-determination. The lower actualities are primarily "physical," which means that they are understandable primarily in terms of their conformity to the past. Their element of "mentality" is simply a confirmation of, or retreat from, the elements received from the past world. The increase in the capacity for enjoyment is accompanied by an increase in mentality, or freedom. The higher actualities have a greater range of appropriated data to synthesize in their process of self-formation. Also, the increase in complexity means an increase in the number of novel real possibilities for actualization. In regard to the finite actuality's relation to God, this means more capacity to disregard the initial aim proferred by God in favor of some other real possibility for that moment of existence. Accordingly, God's stimulation of a more and more complex world, which has the capacity for more and more intrinsic value, means the development of creatures with more and more freedom to reject the divine aims. Increased freedom in relation to the world necessarily means increased freedom in relation to God.

This increased capacity for self-determination is part of the increased capacity for intrinsic and instrumental good and evil, since increased freedom means the capacity to synthesize the data from one's environment in a disharmonious way. Hence, even if the environment in which we find ourselves is not objectively negative, we can make ourselves miserable. Also, we can form ourselves in such a way as to make ourselves objectively destructive elements in the environment of others. We can even do this deliberately—which is the essence of moral evil. Hence, increasing the freedom of the creatures was a risky business on God's part. But it was a necessary risk, if there was to be the chance for greatness.

The fact that this correlation between freedom and intrinsic value is a necessary one, rather than a result of divine arbitrariness, is relevant to one of the central questions discussed in the current literature on the problem of evil. Many theologians and philosophers of religion have proposed a "free-will defense" of God's goodness. The central claim made is that moral evil (which as an evil intention is itself evil, and which in its consequences is the cause of most of the suffering in our world) occurs, because God —even though he is all-good and all-powerful—out of goodness decided to give freedom to human beings. The rationale is that, since freedom is such a great good, God voluntarily gave up all-controlling power, in order to allow us to have genuine freedom and the other values that presuppose it. But there is a serious objection to this theodicy. It takes the form of doubt that freedom is really such an inherently great thing that it is worth running the risk of having creatures such as Hitler. If it were possible to have creatures who could enjoy all the same values which we human beings enjoy, except that they would not really be free, should God not have brought into existence such creatures instead? In other words, if God could have created beings who were like us in every way, except that (a) they always did the best thing, and (b) they *thought* they were only doing this freely, should God not have created these beings instead?

This argument seems convincing, given its premises. But process theology rejects its premises. Since the correlations discussed above are necessary, the hypothetical case is impossible. There could not be beings who would be like us in all respects—i.e., who could enjoy the kinds of values we enjoy, but who would not really be free. Hence, God did not bring about creatures such as us, with our great capacity for discordant self-determination and destructive instrumental value, simply because freedom is in itself a great value, but because beings capable of the values we enjoy must necessarily have these other capacities. The question as to why God did not make sinless robots does not arise. God is partly responsible for most of what we normally call evil, i.e., the evil of discord. Had God not led the realm of finitude out of chaos into a cosmos that includes life, nothing worthy of the term "suffering" would occur. Had God not lured the world on to the creation of beings with the capacity for conscious, rational self-determination, the distinctively human forms of evil on our planet would not occur. Hence, God is responsible for these evils in the sense of having encouraged the world in the direction that made these evils possible. But unnecessary triviality is also evil, since it also detracts from the maximization of enjoyment. Hence, the question as to whether God is indictable for the world's evil reduces to the question as to whether the positive values enjoyed by the higher forms of actuality are worth the risk of the negative values, the sufferings.

The way one answers this question will depend in large part on whether one agrees that overcoming unnecessary triviality is at least as important as avoiding discord.

Some people do not think so. They handle the problem of human existence by minimizing the risk of suffering. They decrease their emotional dependence upon others, both by minimizing the quantity of their significant relations, and by inhibiting as much as possible the natural tendency to respond sympathetically or conformally to others. They choose a more trivial existence than is possible for them, in order to lessen the danger of being hurt.

Since understandings of deity shape ideals for human existence, the above interpretation of the divine purpose behind and in the evolutionary process is relevant to the question of which mode of existence to affirm. Should we risk suffering, in order to have a shot at intense enjoyment? Or should we sacrifice intensity, in order to minimize possible grief? The divine reality, who not only enjoys all enjoyments but also suffers all sufferings, is an Adventurer, choosing the former mode, risking discord in the quest for the various types of perfection that are possible.

How Is an Ecological Attitude Possible?

The expression "ecological attitude" has taken on two central connotations. Strictly speaking, the word "ecology" refers to the study of the interconnections among things, specifically between organisms and their total environments. An "ecological attitude" would thereby be one that recognized the interrelations and hence interdependencies among things. However, "ecology" has taken on an additional connotation, according to which one who has an "ecological attitude" has respect or even reverence for, and perhaps a feeling of kinship with, the other creatures.

Most traditional philosophies and theologies were unecological in both these respects. Being "substance"-oriented, and defining this primarily in terms of independence, they led to habits of thinking and feeling that did not recognize the interdependence of the various levels of existence in general, and of humanity and nature in particular. Accordingly, we are now having to inform ourselves of the fact that ingredients which are harmful to other living things are also harmful to human bodies, on the one hand, and that the health of our psychic life is intimately bound up with the health of our bodily life, on the other. Also, Western modes of thought have tended toward dualism; and those which gained dominance in the seventeenth century were thoroughly dualistic. An absolute line was drawn, explicitly (Descartes) or implicitly, between human beings and other creatures. Only humans had any intrinsic value. The question of the appropriateness of a general attitude of "reverence for life" (Schweitzer) was rarely entertained.

The fact that process thought is ecological in the former sense, that of stressing the mutual dependence of the various levels of enduring individuals, has been adequately stressed. It also supports an ecological attitude in the second sense, in that it attributes the enjoyment of experience to every level of actuality. Things that are supposed to be devoid of the capacity for enjoyment cannot be thought to have any intrinsic value, i.e., value in and for themselves, value that exists independently of some experiencer's imputation of it. Accordingly, we can feel no responsibility to such things. Of course, insofar as such things can have instrumental value for other experiencers, in that they can contribute to their enjoyment, we can rightly feel that we should use them responsibly, i.e., not using up more than our fair share. But we can feel no responsibility to the things themselves—the responsibility is only to the other experiencers, present and future, who could enjoy them.

The belief that all levels of actuality can enjoy some degree of experience provides the basis for a feeling of responsibility directly to them. It is precisely the knowledge that other human beings enjoy experience, and hence have value in and for themselves, that grounds our sense of obligation toward them. This is true even for Kant (who is generally viewed as having a strictly deontological ethic, i.e., one not based upon an anticipation of the values that an ethically right action would create). Thus, one of Kant's formulations of the categorical imperative was that we should treat other human beings as ends in themselves, not merely as means to our own ends. Accordingly, if all actualities, not simply human ones, are constituted by the enjoyment of experience, and hence are to some degree ends in themselves, then we should, to the appropriate degree, treat them as ends and not merely as means to our ends.

Furthermore, the existential implication of recognizing the universality of enjoyment is not simply the extension of moral responsibility. Since God's purpose is the evocation of enjoyment, and since all levels of enjoyment are seen as valued by God, reverence for the neighbor becomes reverence for all creatures. Hence, the double grounds in traditional Christianity for ethical attitudes toward other human beings—the belief that human beings have value for themselves, and that they are valued by God—become in process thought the grounds for ethical attitudes toward all actualities.

Ethical respect for all creatures requires, for any serious implementation, distinctions that have not yet been clarified. Our attitude toward a rock is properly very different from that toward a dog. If these discriminations are not made, undeniable beliefs about reality are flouted. In the first part of this chapter, actual entities and enduring individuals were distinguished, as well as groups of enduring individuals that allowed for the emergence of dominant occasions and thereby souls.

However, there is another way in which several enduring individuals can be ordered. They can be organized as mere aggregates with no unity of experience or enjoyment. The only experiences in the aggregate are the experiences of the actual occasions constituting the various enduring individuals. Rocks, oceans, mountains, beaches, planets, stars, pencils, books, glasses, roads, and corpses are examples. These entities have no coordinated originality of response. Accordingly, the objects of the world that are visible to the human eye, except for living animals, are mere aggregates. As such, they are not higher-level actualities. Hence, their intrinsic value is simply that of the sum of their lowly members.

In other words, while there is no *ontological* dualism between some things that are subjects of experience and other things that are mere objects, there is an *organizational* duality. Those things which *seem* to be mere objects are still affirmed by process thought to *be* mere objects. They are composed of subjects, but they themselves are not subjects. Hence, as such they have no intrinsic value. The only value that needs to be considered (beyond the value of the lowly members, which in most nonliving cases do not depend importantly upon the continued existence of the aggregate) is the instrumental value. In what way does the maximum enjoyment of subjects, present and future, depend on this thing? Of course, included in the instrumental value of a mountain, or a forest, for example, is its aesthetic value.

Plants present a more difficult problem. They are probably best understood as aggregates. This was at least Whitehead's view, as he said: "A tree is a democracy." (*AI* 264.) This means that a plant's apparently coordinated behavior is understandable in terms of similar movements of the majority of cells in the various parts of the plant. Hence, there would be no center of enjoyment in the plant higher than the individual cells. However, the survival of the member cells depends upon the survival of the plant. Hence, in considering the justifiability of destroying plants one should not consider only their external instrumental value (positive and negative), but also their instrumental value in supporting their members.

This distinction between the two major types of organization does much to bring the process view of reality into harmony with our "common sense." However, there is another obvious question. We need to act. And virtually every action is destructive of life. How can we have reverence for all experiential wholes, at least all living ones, and continue to live? And how could we, for example, justify killing a malarial mosquito, or even a group of cancerous cells, to save a human life, if we are supposed to have equal reverence for all life?

The key word in this question is "equal." There is nothing in the process view to suggest that we should have equal reverence for all actualities, even all living ones. True, some ecological writers have advocated a "democracy of value," which would seemingly entail equal reverence. And Albert Schweitzer refused to work out a theoretical justification for choosing the life of human beings, which he as a doctor tried to save, over the lives of the lower organisms that he sought to destroy (although he stated that in practice we must make this choice). But as the two previous sections made clear, there is a hierarchy of values; so when a choice must be made, there is a basis for discriminating value judgments. Destroying the life of some types of actualities is more serious than destroying that of others. Everything else being equal, those with greater intrinsic value are to be preferred, when a choice must be made.

Of course, everything else is rarely equal. For, besides the intrinsic value of things, we must consider their instrumental value, the role they play in the total ecosystem. The instrumental value of things varies greatly. Also, we still understand relatively little about the mutual interdependencies of the various types of enduring individuals. The relativity view of time, which defines the future as everything that is affected by the present, means that things have extremely long-run effects! Accordingly, working out an ecological ethic will be a gigantic undertaking. The main point of the present section is that process thought provides the theoretical basis for such an ethic.

5

HUMAN EXISTENCE

PROCESS THEOLOGY AND
EXISTENTIAL ANTHROPOLOGY

During the formative period of recent process theology, the thought of Rudolf Bultmann was in the ascendancy. Theologians influenced by Whitehead and Hartshorne found much of Bultmann's work highly congenial. Process theologians, too, wanted to demythologize inherited forms of thought and to translate them into modern terms. They, too, believed it particularly important to avoid treating the human subject as an object, and to employ categories appropriate to human subjects. They, too, found the *Existenzialien* of Heidegger persuasive and fruitful for this purpose. They objected only that Bultmann did not develop his theology in tandem with his anthropology, and that God also should be spoken of as subject in appropriate ways.

Schubert Ogden was the leader in this move to wed the anthropology of Heidegger and Bultmann with the understanding of God of Whitehead and Hartshorne. The wedding was remarkably successful because of the extensive similarities between Whitehead and Heidegger in their analysis of human subjects. Heidegger's account was fuller and more specifically focused on the distinctively human and in this respect had a great advantage. Hence, without inconsistency Ogden could use Heidegger and Bultmann in the context of a process theology.

Central to existential thought is the formal doctrine that existence precedes essence. What we are as human beings is not decided for us by God, by society, or by our personal past. We decide in the act of existing. We may try to evade the radical responsibility that this places upon us, but such evasion is itself a decision as to what we are. Furthermore, there are no preestablished rules that either factually or normatively govern our existence. Each situation is unique. If we choose to apply a rule, that is the choice for which we are responsible. There is no predetermined end toward which we are directed. The future is radically open. We create the future in our decision. We are responsible for the future. To all this a Whiteheadian agrees.

Furthermore, our existence is radically contingent—we might not have been. There is no preexistent plan that includes us and assigns us a role in the scheme of things. In Heidegger's words, we experience ourselves as "thrown" into the world. It is in this arbitrary situation that we must assume responsibility for ourselves. With this, too, a Whiteheadian can agree.

Our existence is a being-in-the-world. There is no self apart from the world or world apart from the self, but the one reality of being-in-the-world. Our existence is not simply located in our bodies or our heads. The world belongs to it as it belongs to the world. With this too a Whiteheadian agrees, for an actual occasion cannot be abstracted from its actual world, nor an actual world from the occasion of which it is the actual world.

All this one could learn as well from Whitehead as from Heidegger. But Heidegger went on to make his important distinction of the two modes of being-in-the-world. One is the inauthentic mode in which one's projects are set for one by others—by social expectations or past conditioning or the hope of reward. The second is the authentic mode in which one chooses one's own projects. This distinction commended itself to Bultmann for the interpretation of Paul's view of unbelief and faith. And through Bultmann it became widely influential in theology. The distinction did not arise readily out of Whitehead's thought, but it could be understood by a Whiteheadian. In this sense it was grafted into process theology.

Process theologians still have much to learn from existentialism, and the alliance of process theology with existential theology has left a permanent mark. But from the beginning there were tensions between them. For example Heidegger pictures human existence or *Dasein* as being-toward-death. This highlights his view of human existence as a single entity from birth to death. Whitehead, however, pictures human existence as a sequence of moments. For him, we who live are dying constantly. In his own words, we are "perpetually perishing." Of course the whole series will come to an end, and that is an important consideration. But the meaning of our existence must be forged in the teeth of the more fundamental fact of perpetual perishing.

This difference is connected with a difference in the conception of relations to others. For Heidegger, the other human being appears only as the one who shares the world *(Mitsein)*. This is inevitable, since there can be no real internal relations between people. For Whitehead, however, the difference between my relation to my own past and future and my relation to others is not absolute. Of course it is important. But the other can be a contributory element in the constitution of my own existence, and I can contribute to the other. We can be bound together in a real mutuality. Whitehead does not accept the lonely isolation of each human being affirmed by Heidegger as ultimately real and to be fully realized by meditating upon the solitude of death. Instead, Whitehead affirms that we exist first of all in community and establish relative independence within it. With Tillich he holds that participation and individuality are polar, so that the more we participate with others in community the more we can become individuals, and the more we become individuals, the more richly we participate in community. It is the view of isolated self-identity from birth to death that is the illusion.

The focus upon the human to the exclusion of the divine that has disturbed Ogden in Bultmann's theology was complemented by the neglect of nature, including the human body. For the existentialist, nature could be only the world that being was in. The phenomenological method did not allow consideration of nature's own reality as analogous in some way to the being-in-the-world of human existence. But for Whitehead, dogs, amoebae, and even electrons are also best conceived as instances of being-in-the-world. The actual world of each existing thing is in turn a community of entities each of which is a being-in-the-world. And God is the supreme instance of being-in-the-world. This places human existence, so brilliantly analyzed by the existentialists, in a quite different context of understanding.

While Whitehead shares the existentialist stress on decision and responsibility, it is not for him the dominant note. Also decision is not so heavily freighted with moral considerations. The decision is directed toward a "satisfaction." The occasion "enjoys" its own immediacy. It attains some measure of "harmony," "intensity," "truth," and "beauty."

Although the future is open for Heidegger and Bultmann, they lack the note of the *Novum*, the qualitatively new. For Whitehead, on the other hand, creative novelty is of the essence of the future to which one is open, and the future has this openness not simply because human decisions are not predecided, but because the radically new cannot be anticipated. The Whiteheadian can live with a hope or expectancy foreign to the existentialist but close to Ernst Bloch.

There is a difference also in the feeling for the past. For a Whiteheadian, as for Bultmann, it is meaningful to think of liberation from the past. The tendency to conform to or reenact one's past can deepen habits that are inappropriate to the new situation. To be free from the past is to be able to respond to the new possibility given in the new moment. This is supremely important. But for Whitehead the new possibility is the opportunity to incorporate the past in a new way. There is no moment that is not constituted by its synthesis of elements from the past. If to be free from the past were to exclude the past, the present would be entirely vacuous. The power of the new is that it makes possible a greater inclusion of elements from the past that otherwise would prove incompatible and exclude each other from their potential contribution. Where the existentialist seems to see an antithesis between having the moment controlled by the past and allowing the future to be determinative, Whitehead says that the more effective the future is, the more fully the potential contribution of the past is realized.

Finally, there are contrasting views of human historicity. Bultmann stresses that human existence is historical in the sense of *geschichtlich.* That means we are agents of decision in relation to an open future. But it is not *historisch,* that is, it is not to be understood in terms of the outwardly changing course of events. Accordingly, the question of how human existence emerged from prehuman forms does not arise, and the stages of its development are barely acknowledged. As a result, Bultmann can affirm that the Christ event changed the situation for human existence only by introducing ad hoc the idea of a unique act of God. Whitehead can agree with what is said of human existence as *geschichtlich,* but for him it is also evident that the human existence we know emerged through several stages from prehuman animal forms of existence. To understand ourselves, and also the diversities of forms of human existence today, this evolutionary-historical character of existence should be recognized.

Whitehead considers the emergence of the human from its animal background in terms of the role of novelty, language, and religion. In each case he sees discontinuity within continuity, but the discontinuity is of such importance that he recognizes a qualitative change. In relation to novelty, he writes: "Animal life can face conventional novelties with conventional devices. But the governing principle lacks large power for the sudden introduction of any major novelty." (*MT* 35.) But "when we come to mankind, nature seems to have burst through another of its boundaries. The central activity of enjoyment and expression has assumed a reversal in the importance of its diverse functionings. The conceptual entertainment of unrealized possibility becomes a major factor in human mentality." (*MT* 36.)

Language is also distinctive of human beings. It is so important that Whitehead can write "that the mentality of mankind and the language of mankind created each other." (*MT* 57.) But here too there are prehuman anticipations. Speech in its embryonic form "varies between emotional expression and signalling." (*MT* 52.)

And this form of speech is found in animals as well as human beings.

Even with respect to religion, Whitehead traces a history of discontinuity in continuity. Since religion is not simply one aspect of human existence among many, but the organization of the interior life, the history of religion is the inner development of human beings that supervenes upon the completion of the biological-evolutionary process.

The four factors in religion are ritual, emotion, belief, and rationalization. (*RM* 18.) Ritual "can be discerned in the animals." It "may be defined as the habitual performance of definite actions which have no direct relevance to the preservation of the physical organisms of the actors." (*RM* 20.) It "is the primitive outcome of superfluous energy and leisure." (*RM* 20.)

Ritual excites emotion, and "mankind became artists in ritual." (*RM* 21.) "Emotions sensitize the organism. Thus the unintended effect was produced of sensitizing the human organism in a variety of ways diverse from what would have been produced by the necessary work of life." (*RM* 21.)

Belief supervened upon ritual and its accompanying emotion. Myths arose to explain the ritual and the emotion and to accentuate the emotion. "Religion, in this stage of belief, marks a new formative agent in the ascent of man. For just as ritual encouraged *emotion* beyond the mere response to practical necessities, so religion in this further stage begets *thoughts* divorced from the mere battling with the pressure of circumstances. Imagination secured in it a machinery for its development; thought has been led beyond the immediate objects in sight." (*RM* 27.)

This emergence of thought initiated in its turn the rationalization of belief, which has occurred within the past six thousand years. In the thousand years before Christ the process accelerated and rational religion was born. "Rational religion is religion whose beliefs and rituals have been reorganized with the aim of making it the central element in a coherent ordering of life—an ordering which shall be coherent both in respect to the elucidation of thought, and in respect to the direction of conduct towards a unified purpose commanding ethical approval." (*RM* 31.) Christianity and Buddhism are two contrasting but equally developed rational religions.

Four points can be noted from these observations. First, history is interpreted most fundamentally as a history of modes of subjective existence rather than of the rise and fall of empires or other external events. Second, the history of existence is bound up with the history of religion. Third, the course of events is natural in the sense of being continuous and intelligible. One change creates a situation in which another can occur. Fourth, the course of events gives rise to diverse forms at the same level of development. Not all differences are to be placed on a single scale.

STRUCTURES OF HUMAN EXISTENCE

Existentialists have provided a powerful and illuminating analysis of the post-Christian structure of existence. Whitehead has shown that an evolutionary philosophy can trace the development of human subjectivity as well as of physiological changes. This suggestion that the present structure of existence arose out of earlier structures opens the way to a history of structures of human existence. Also, instead of viewing other cultures as particular expressions of the one structure of existence discovered through careful phenomenological analysis of current Western existence, we can be open to discovering their own distinctive structures. In such a context the role of historical figures such as Buddha, Socrates, and Jesus can be seen as bringing new structures of existence into being. Bultmann's belief that through Jesus' death and resurrection a change was effected in the human situation at this most fundamental level can be examined as a historical hypothesis without introducing any ad hoc notions of a unique act of God.

In the preceding chapter the earlier stages of evolutionary development were traced in terms of the emergence of new structures or organisms. Most important is the emergence of animals with central nervous systems supporting higher-grade occasions of experience. The evolutionary function of these "dominant" or "presiding" occasions was to unify sensory data about the world external to the animal organism, data relevant to the survival and well-being of the organism, and to trigger appropriate motor responses.

These dominant occasions of animal experience could occur only sporadically or they could occur continuously over long periods of time. In some instances they integrated very limited parts of the experience of the body and exercised but little influence upon it. In other cases they played a much more thorough role of synthesis and control. The evolutionary direction was toward increased centralization. Whitehead describes the animal with a central nervous system, and hence a series of presiding occasions, as a "monarchical society."

Presiding or dominant occasions can come into being almost entirely out of the events in the body, but never wholly so. Every occasion takes account of its entire world, and that world includes past occasions of unified experience as well as the body. The question is one of degree of importance of the past experiences in informing new ones. This ranges from trivial to primary. As the importance increases, learning becomes a factor in the occasions of animal experience. That is, what is experienced now takes account of the past experiences of that particular animal.

The evolutionary function of centralized animal experience was to promote the survival and well-being of the animal body. However, every occasion of experience also aims at its own enjoyment. The relative weight of its own enjoyment and of that of its relevant future, in this case the body, varies. Further, as the animal experience is increasingly shaped by experiences of previous presiding occasions, it increasingly aims at enhancing the enjoyment of succeeding occasions in this series as well. The contrast between the aim to achieve enjoyment at the level of unified experience and the aim to achieve the well-being of the animal body is not sharp, for the enjoyment of the dominant animal experience arises out of the bodily enjoyment and in turn contributes to it. But the dominant occasions can entertain aims that transcend the needs of the body, and where they exercise considerable control and have established an important continuity through time, they may employ the body for their own purposes. At this point we may speak of the animal "psyche" or "soul."

Even in highly developed animals, the psyche functions to serve the needs of the body. The psyche's autonomous enjoyment, that is, its enjoyment beyond that derived from the body's enjoyment, is generally slight. But once the psyche is established with the capacity for autonomous enjoyment, the degree of importance of that enjoyment can increase. It can become the major end of the self-actualization of the occasions of psychic experience, and the well-being of the body can become its aim chiefly as that is instrumental to its own enjoyment. This is the situation that prevails in the human species. The shift from a psyche primarily serving the body, to a psyche primarily using the body for its own purposes, is a major threshold crossing in the evolutionary-historical process. Once that threshold is crossed, primary interest attaches to the structure of the inner life of the psyche itself rather than to that of the psychophysical organism. From this point on we can speak of "structures of existence."

Animal experience introduced consciousness into the world. Consciousness selected for attention those features of the environment that constituted either danger or food and appropriate motor responses were triggered accordingly. Consciousness continued to function in this way also for human beings, but in them it also highlighted psychic activities of another sort prompted by the psyche's aim at its own enjoyment. These were symbolic activities intensifying emotion and not governed by practical necessities. These constituted the original center of human existence, and although their results were consciously experienced, as psychic activities they were unconscious and prethematized.

In the history of human existence, consciousness functions in relation to nonconscious experience somewhat as, in the history of prehuman structures, the dominant animal occasions functioned in relation to the body. Consciousness is not the primary element in constituting the psychic life, but it plays an increasing role within this life. As the role of consciousness increases, it becomes the focus of the aim for enjoyment. Finally, it becomes the center from which the rest of the psychic life is perceived.

In human beings consciousness plays a role it did not play in their prehuman ancestry. It tests the results of the free play of psychic activities against the world it highlights in sense experience. In this way it disciplines the nonconscious imaginative life. This disciplining of the imagination is rationality, and it is this rationalizing activity of consciousness that finally establishes itself as primary for some segment of the human population. The ascendancy of the rational consciousness and the reordering of the inner life to conform with it constituted the crossing of another major threshold in the historical development of structures of existence. Whitehead calls it the emergence of "rational religion." Karl Jaspers calls it the "axial revolution." Both date it in the first millennium B.C., and Jaspers calls attention to its independent occurrence in China, India, Persia, Greece, and Israel.

The emergence of new structures of existence is in one sense always progress, but this progress is bought at a high price. Today there are serious questions as to whether the price was too high, and whether progress is not chiefly to be seen as a disease. Norman Brown *(Life Against Death)* calls attention to the superior health and naturalness of the animal whose bodily existence is primary over its psyche, and calls for "the resurrection of the body." There is no doubt but that when the psyche subordinated the body to its own purposes it introduced an element of dis-ease from which we have suffered increasingly ever since. Many religious teachers call us to recover the primal harmony with the body that was lost with the "fall" of the human species into primarily psychic life.

This fall was greatly accentuated through the axial revolution. Despite the primacy of the psyche in all human beings, the central activity of the psyche was in its nonconscious and prethematized experience. This was intimately influenced by the body and in many respects conformal to it. Further, it was also intimately influenced by the other members of the tribal community, the natural environment of the tribe, and the divine reality, which we all unconsciously experience. Thus in primitive or tribal existence, the human being participated in a larger community of beings—things, people and the divine—of which the body was an important part. But when the long process of rationalizing experience reached its completion in the axial revolution, the self was estranged from this wider community. The sense of the divine reality faded or disappeared from consciousness. The environment, including both the body and other people, was sharply distinguished from the self whose seat was now in the rationalized consciousness. There was enormous increase of individuality and personal freedom. But there was an enormous loss of participation and thus of support from a wider community of beings. The rational religions that arose in the axial period were at once the vehicles of this deepening of the "fall" and ways of salvation from its consequences. Each shaped a distinct structure of existence, and these axial structures of existence constitute even today the major alternatives for human existence. We will focus upon those which arose in India and in Israel.

In India the individual isolation caused by the emergence of the self in the rationalized consciousness was felt with peculiar intensity. The Indian sense of the endless ongoingness of the world process and of the self's involvement with it through an endless succession of lives undoubtedly contributed to this. The leading thinkers undertook to clarify the self's situation so as to point a way of release from misery. Their thought characteristically revolved about the body, the psyche (in the sense used here of the actual flow of individual experience), and the self. Far from attempting to recover the unity of the self with the body and with others which had been lost through the human and axial revolutions, their analyses furthered the separation by strengthening the identification of the self with rational consciousness. Release was sought by a separation or distinction of the self from the empirical psyche which, through its involvement with the body and its own time-bound desires, perpetuated the self's bondage.

Of the many analyses and remedies two types stand out. Some sages believed that the self was actually corrupted by its involvement in the psychic and physical worlds and that the need was to purify it, usually through ascetic practices. Other sages believed that the self was in fact always pure, and that the task was to realize that in truth it had nothing to do with the corrupted worlds of the body and psyche. They developed forms of psychic discipline that could facilitate the existential realization of this intellectually apprehended truth. Of the latter schools the most important is Advaita Vedanta, which taught that the true self is not an individuated entity over against other selves. It does not participate in the individuating features of the psychic life with which it falsely identifies itself. In its completely undifferentiated reality it is one with the reality that underlies the flux of forms that constitutes the psychic and the physical worlds. This is expressed in the famous formula that Atman and Brahman are one, i.e., that the self and the universal sacred reality are identical. Both are unchangeable, pure, and perfect. The task is not to achieve transcendence of change and process but to realize existentially that one is already always perfect. In this realization lies release from dis-ease.

Gautama's enlightenment led him in a different direction. The sense of self is constituted, he saw, by the sense of identity through time. Memory of one's past and anticipation of one's future binds one to that past and future. The view that the particular past and future are in fact one's own implies that there is a self that endures through them. This is the basis of remorse and anxiety as well as desire or craving. But there is in fact no self-identical self which is the subject of a succession of experiences. The identity through time is not a given reality about which beliefs are entertained. It exists only in being believed. I am the same self now as yesterday if I view certain events that occurred yesterday as my private past. I am the same self now that I will be tomorrow if I view certain anticipated occurrences tomorrow as happening to me. But there is no metaphysical ground for these identifications. The reality is a flux of happenings with no substantial ground. When that is realized existentially there is release, or rather there is the recognition that there is nothing to be released.

The course of events in Israel was quite different. There was no sophisticated discussion of self, psyche, and body, and there were no physical and psychic techniques developed for the purification of the self or the realization of the purity or nonexistence of the self. There was instead a vivid experience of a male tribal deity, Yahweh, and his requirements, and a progressive rationalization of this experience. This rationalization led to the thought of God as the great "I" who created the world and rightfully claimed the obedience of his people. This in turn led to the understanding of the people as respondents to this claim who could choose for or against it. As it was realized that the decision is finally made by individuals, there arose a sense of the personal self as deciding how to act in relation to the divine will. The divine will was progressively rationalized into ethical laws governing interpersonal behavior. As a result the human person became a *rational will* fully responsible for how he or she behaved toward others.

The ethical structure of existence brought into being in this way has played a large role in the West through Judaism, Christianity, Islam, and ethical humanism. In wide circles it still constitutes the basis for commonsense views of what life is all about. One exists as a free agent choosing between the rightful claims of ethical principles and inferior goals chiefly dictated by excessive self-concern. The self or "I" is thus constituted as the agent of choice which can be called the rational will. Emotions are real and important, but they are distinct from the self. They may support the self or threaten the self, but it is the self's responsibility not to be swayed by them away from rational, ethical decision. Theoretical and speculative thought may be appropriate activities, but when and how they are appropriate is to be decided by the self as rational will. They do not constitute the self. The self as rational will endures through time, accepting responsibility for its past acts and anticipating future ones. Whatever pain is experienced in this mode of selfhood is to be accepted.

Primitive Christianity emerged out of this ethical structure of existence. It simultaneously intensified this existence and transformed it. Existence as rational will requires that what is ethically demanded is within the control of the will. To demand what one cannot do is an absurdity. The demands may be extremely exacting, as in the Pharisaic law, but in principle obedience is, and must be, possible. This means that the requirements of God are tailored to the capacities of the rational will.

The primary sphere of control of the rational will is outer action. By refusing to be swayed by emotions and personal preferences, ethical persons can so act as to benefit others and support the structure of an ongoing society. They can even act in ways that will have a favorable effect upon their inner life. But they cannot control their feelings in the way that they control their behavior. Primitive Christianity was not satisfied by these limits and expressed the demand that action for others go beyond calculative ethical behavior and express the motivation of love. In other words, one's feelings as well as one's outer actions were brought within the realm of responsibility. One identified with one's aspirations for a fuller righteousness than the rational will could support. Hence, Christianity rejected the identification of the ultimate center of existence with the rational will. The self can exist only as a distancing of itself from the will, as well as from emotion and reason, and this implies a sense of responsibility for all of these dimensions of experience. This self can be called *spirit*.

The spiritual structure of existence is more difficult to articulate than the ethical one. One avenue to understanding it is to note the rise of autobiographical accounts of the inner life in the sphere of its effectiveness. The self as spirit examines itself. In this sense it objectifies and transcends itself. As self-objectifying or self-transcending existence it is profoundly unstable, for spiritual self-examination alters the nature of the self that is examined. The self-examination both expresses the sense of responsibility for self and produces that responsibility. But the self cannot control itself in the way that the rational will can control outward behavior. Thus the self aspiring for a new righteousness is frustrated in its efforts to transform itself into what it should be. "Ought" does not imply "can" in spiritual existence in the direct way that is true of ethical existence. Just for this reason the sense of "original sin" or "natural depravity" comes into play to describe the resistance of the spirit to the realization of its own aspirations.

Like the existence analyzed by the existentialists, the structure of spiritual existence can be actualized in two modes. However, the German terms *eigentlich* and *uneigentlich* do not fit them. These terms, translated into English as authentic and inauthentic, refer to living in terms of one's own proper purposes or in terms of purposes established for one by others, respectively. The alternatives for the Christian are different. The two modes are love and self-preoccupation.

The peculiar danger of spiritual existence is that the self that objectifies or transcends itself becomes preoccupied with itself in a self-enclosed way. It narcissistically wallows in its own guilt and its own achievements. Spontaneous affection and spontaneous ethical obedience give way to actions motivated by reflexive concern for their effect upon the spiritual person. By continually asking whether its motives are pure, the self destroys the possibility of this purity. In this way spirit can make of itself an isolated existence intolerable to itself and to others. This is the peculiar possibility for dis-ease introduced by spiritual existence.

The alternative is the Christian mode of spiritual existence in which the spirit is open to the creative-responsive love of God. The sense of responsibility for one's self is retained in its fullness, but the self is also open to receiving that which it cannot attain of itself. In its openness to the creative love of God, the self receives new possibilities for its own existence that point it away from itself toward wider horizons of interest. Through its openness to the responsive love of God, it receives assurance of its acceptance in spite of its sin, is freed from preoccupation with itself, and is enabled to turn to others with a disinterested concern for their welfare. The openness to God's love also enables the Christian to be sensitively responsive to the feelings of others. In all these ways spiritual existence, freed from self-preoccupation by openness to God, is peculiarly capable of reflecting the creative-responsive love of God in its relation to others. This loving mode of existence is the peculiar possibility for increased enjoyment introduced by spiritual existence.

6

JESUS CHRIST

To complete five chapters of a book on Christian theology with scarcely a mention of Christ appears to give evidence for a criticism often leveled against process theology. Critics charge that it is really philosophy and not theology at all. Process theologians deny this charge, but their writings testify to a different judgment from that of their critics as to the appropriate way to write theology today. We judge that Christian meaning can best be made alive today through a truly contemporary vision of the world that is at the same time truly Christian. We are not so much concerned that the forms and language of the past be preserved as that the faith come fully to life in relation to our needs and opportunities. Whitehead seems to us at once to provide a brilliant contemporary vision and to make our faith live in a new way.

In one sense, then, this chapter is not the beginning of the presentation of process Christology. Instead it will show that Christ has permeated the preceding chapters. What has been said about God is already Christological in two ways. First, as Whitehead recognized, his understanding of God is indebted to the life and insights of Jesus. Second, the creative love of God, insofar as it is incarnate, *is* Christ. What has been said about the world, and especially about human beings, has been said in the light of that Christological doctrine of God.

The chapter begins with a summary of Whitehead's direct contributions to our reflection about Jesus and about incarnation. It proceeds with an explanation of Christ as creative transformation and of the relation of Jesus to Christ. It concludes with brief comments on the church as the Body of Christ and on the Trinity.

WHITEHEAD ON
JESUS AND INCARNATION

Whitehead viewed Jesus from the perspective of a keenly interested philosophical historian who recognized indebtedness to him. He saw Jesus as a supreme figure of history. Furthermore, history has authority, for all the richness and depth of our insights is derived from past figures. "The appeal to history is the appeal to summits of attainment beyond any immediate clarity in our own individual existence. It is an appeal to authority." (*AI* 208.) In the case of religion the appeal is to "the supernormal experience of mankind in its moments of finest insight." (*RM* 32.)

In contrast with Buddhism, which began with the teaching of the way to enlightenment, Christianity began with the life of Jesus. As this was told, it had elements that "have evoked a response from all that is best in human nature. The Mother, the Child, and the bare manger; the lowly man, homeless and self-forgetful, with his message of peace, love, and sympathy: the suffering, the agony, the tender words as life ebbed, the final despair: and the whole with the authority of supreme victory." (*AI* 214.) "The life of Christ is not an exhibition of over-ruling power. Its glory is for those who can discern it, and not for the world. Its power lies in its absence of force. It has the decisiveness of a supreme idea." (*RM* 57.) This idea, of a supreme power that is persuasive and not coercive, had been attained by Plato, waveringly, late in his life. "The power of Christianity lies in its revelation in act of that which Plato divined in theory." (*AI* 214.)

Jesus' message dwelt upon "the tender elements in the world, which slowly and in quietness operate by love." (*PR* 520.) Through him Christians were led to affirm God's immanence in the world. But he did not express his teaching in theoretical form. His reported sayings "are not formularized thought. They are descriptions of direct insight. The ideas are in his mind as immediate pictures, and not as analyzed in terms of abstract concepts. . . . His sayings are actions and not adjustments of concepts. He speaks in the lowest abstractions that language is capable of, if it is to be language at all and not the fact itself." (*RM* 56–57.)

Jesus' teaching expresses a boundless naïveté (*RM* 56) possible only in the peasant community of Galilee. It was as irrelevant to the actual problems of power and order in the Roman Empire as it is in our own time. Precisely because of its impracticality it has constituted a standard that is "a gauge by which to test the defects of human society. So long as the Galilean images are but dreams of an unrealized world, so long they must spread the infection of an uneasy spirit." (*AI* 20–21.) Just because of the concreteness of the images, their radical and impractical meaning cannot be concealed. Over the centuries they have altered the structures of society.

These comments express Whitehead's deep appreciation of Jesus and respect for his authority. He leaves open the equal importance of analogous events occurring elsewhere. But he does hold that Plato's insight and Jesus' life embody the greatest advances in the expression of moral "intuition which mark the growth of recent civilization." (*AI* 212.) Because of Jesus' embodiment of a supreme ideal, "the history of the world divides at this point of time." (*RM* 57.)

The subsequent story of theological interpretation and development also interested Whitehead. In the schools of Antioch and Alexandria the finest minds of the day struggled to understand the kinds of relations that existed between God and Jesus and among the members of the Trinity. The Platonic philosophy with which they worked had no satisfactory concepts. Plato answered the question of how God and the Ideas are in the world in terms of dramatic imitation. The Christian thinkers believed in a mutual immanence of the members of the Trinity in each other, a real incarnation of God in Jesus, and a direct immanence of God in the world in general. In affirming the real immanence of one entity in another entity "these Christian theologians have the distinction of being the only thinkers who in a fundamental metaphysical doctrine have improved upon Plato." (*AI* 215.) This doctrine of real internal relations between entities is generalized by Whitehead and is one of the central themes of his philosophy of organism.

CHRIST AS
CREATIVE TRANSFORMATION

Like many liberal Christians, Whitehead used "Christ" synonymously with "Jesus." But in the orthodox doctrine and in the imaginative life of Christendom, Christ is also God, especially as creatively and redemptively incarnate in the world. Whitehead's philosophy opens to the theologian fresh possibilities for reflecting on the divine incarnation. This process was begun in Chapter 1, and was continued in the discussion of God as creative love in Chapter 3. It remains for us in this section to see where God as creative love is to be discerned in the course of events.

In Chapter 3, God as creative love was identified with the Primordial Nature of God. God, in this aspect, is the source of novel order and ordered novelty in the world. Although in this vision a shift has been made from static to dynamic order and from order as such to order with novelty, what is spoken of is what the Church Fathers called the Logos. As explained in Chapter 3, the Primordial Nature, or Logos, is present or incarnate in creatures as the initial aim in relation to which the creature decides how to constitute itself. The initial aim is at that form of actualization which achieves the greatest enjoyment immediately for the occasion and for the subsequent occasions it will affect.

The *incarnate* Logos is Christ. In this broadest sense, Christ is present in all things. But two qualifications are in order. First, although there is no absolute line between the inanimate and the animate worlds, in the former the presence of the Logos is barely distinguishable from the repetition of the past. It is in living things that the proper work of the Logos is significantly manifest. Second, as we deal with those higher organisms in which the work of the Logos is especially to be discerned, the decision of the creature becomes increasingly important. This means that the extent of the effectiveness of the Logos in these creatures is largely decided by the creature. Christ is present to a greater or lesser extent as the creature decides for or against the Logos. Christ is most fully present in human beings when they are most fully open to that presence.

In each moment the human subject is given an actual world with innumerable discordant elements. There is no way in which all of these elements can be united in a single experience. The easiest way to achieve a new synthesis is by blocking out altogether the discordant elements. The result is a trivial harmony lacking in intensity or strength. Whitehead speaks of this as "anaesthesia."

There is another possibility. Although the discordant elements cannot be brought into harmony just as they stand, there may be a larger, more inclusive novel pattern in which they can both be contained, in such a way that the contrast between them contributes to the intensity of the whole. But this pattern is not part of the given world of the new occasion. It comes from the Primordial Nature of God, or the Logos. Insofar as this pattern is embodied, the occasion is creatively transformed in relation to its predecessors. Mutually exclusive elements in its world become effective contrasts contributing to the strength of beauty—that is, the enjoyment—of the whole.

An illustration will help to give substance to these statements. A young man holds strictly to conservative moral principles. He becomes a part of a group in which carefree and casual behavior with respect to morals is favored. He can respond in several ways. First, he may simply shut out from reflection the conflicting ideas, avoiding discussion or a decision between them. This is the way of anaesthesia. Second, he may, after reflection, decide simply to adhere to the conservative moral principles, excluding the threat involved in his new awareness that there are other possibilities. Third, he may simply abandon his past views and accept those of his new friends. Fourth, he may compromise, retaining strict principles in some respects and adopting a carefree attitude in others. In none of these responses does novelty play any significant role. Changes are involved in some of them, but the changes are simply redistribution of existing elements.

There is a fifth possibility. He may perceive that both moral rigor and carefree spontaneity have their value from a larger perspective that understands and appreciates both. This larger perspective will be enriched by their inclusion and the quality of experience that embodies it will be stronger or more intense. In this case something genuinely new has been introduced. What before were mutually exclusive elements are now contrasts that jointly contribute to the whole. He has not abandoned his own past convictions; but by being set into a new and larger context these convictions are creatively transformed.

Creative transformation is the essence of growth, and growth is of the essence of life. Growth is not achieved by merely adding together elements in the given world in different combinations. It requires the transformation of those elements through the introduction of novelty. It alters their nature and meaning without suppressing or destroying them. The source of the novelty is the Logos, whose incarnation is Christ. Where Christ is effectively present, there is creative transformation.

Creative transformation is involved in all human responsive love. To love another person in this way is to allow that person's feelings to affect oneself. But those feelings, as different from one's own, cannot be simply added to them. Ordinarily, in order to protect ourselves, we largely shut out the feelings of others from any rich contribution to our experience. Occasionally we are overwhelmed by alien feelings in such a way as to lose our own integrity. But it is also possible, by a certain distancing of ourselves both from our own feelings and from those of the other, to enter into a novel mode of being in which both operate with their own integrity in a larger whole that is enriched by their contrasts. Good counselors must in this way be genuinely sensitive to the feelings of their counselees without losing themselves in them. Only as both are retained in a larger whole is the counselee helped. But that involves novelty and the creative transformation of the counselor.

Creative transformation is involved also in all human creative love. The creative love of God produces creative transformation in creatures. One major direction of that transformation is toward the broadening of the anticipation of the future that is to be affected by one's actions. This broadening of horizons does not destroy interest in one's private future or in that of those with whom one is more immediately concerned, but it sets these narrower concerns in a wider context within which they are transformed. The interest in the larger whole puts interest in more limited aspects of the future in a new light and gives them a new role. The person in whom creative love completes its work in this way is creatively transformed. Thus Christ is the giver of both responsive and creative human love.

Although the ultimate locus of creative transformation is always the individual occasion of experience, its effects are publicly manifest in human creations. Original thinking in science and philosophy, original art in all its forms, original styles of life and social organizations, all witness to the peculiarly effective presence of Christ. All involve a novelty that is not mere change but the creative transformation of what is received from the past. None of these are to be seen as pure and unambiguous instances of Christ's presence. Nor is it always clear whether a true breakthrough has occurred or whether there is simply a change in the arrangement of materials. But the history of science, philosophy, art, life-styles, and social organization is the history of repeated creative transformations.

This means that Christ is in no wise limited to the sphere of "the religious" as this is conventionally understood. He is not limited to the church or to those places where he is named and acknowledged. But this does not mean that his work is unaffected by the way he is understood and received. Christ is present in those who deny that there are any unrealized possibilities and who believe that everything that happens is settled by what has happened in the past; but those beliefs tend to reduce the effectiveness of his presence. Christ works in those who confuse him with static moral principles, but there too his presence is truncated. Christ can be most fully present and effective where people believe in creative transformation, understand it rightly, trust it, and open themselves to it. This is most likely to happen when the effective presence of the Logos is recognized as Christ. These are exemplifications of the general principle, discussed in Chapter 2, as to how conscious beliefs emphasize selected features of prethematized experience and thereby affect human existence.

CHRIST AND JESUS

To name creative transformation Christ is implicitly to assert that it is peculiarly related to Jesus. This may not be immediately apparent, although we have noted the indebtedness to Jesus of Whitehead's account of the Logos as God in his Primordial Nature. We need to show that not only is this understanding of God's incarnate presence in the world historically indebted to Jesus, but also that the working of God in this way was furthered by him.

The preceding chapter showed that Jesus' impact brought into history a distinctive structure of existence centering around a self-objectifying or self-transcending self. This spiritual structure could lead to self-preoccupation, but in its Christian form it is open to God's love and thereby also to the neighbor's need. The self-objectifying structure of existence is peculiarly open to repeated creative transformation; for it is characteristically by placing what one has been and thought in a new perspective that it is retained in a new and more inclusive whole. This creative transformation will be resisted where self-objectification leads to self-preoccupation, but where one believes in and accepts God's love the process is rendered full and continuous. Thus Christ is peculiarly present in Christian existence.

Another way of seeing Jesus as furthering creative transformation is in terms of his revelatory significance. The vision of reality that is expressed through the sayings and actions of Jesus is one in which the primary reality with which we have to do is the creative-responsive love of God. Insofar as we genuinely receive Jesus as the revelation of the basic truth about reality, we are more open to the divine impulses in our experience. We experience this element as more important than we otherwise would, and we are more apt to respond positively to it. In this way, accepting Jesus as the decisive revelation of what the divine reality is like opens us to being creatively transformed.

To understand the importance of revelation in this way, and to consider the distinctiveness of Christian existence, are peculiarly modern ways of viewing the "work" of Jesus. In the early church it was seen chiefly in two other ways. Paul understood the Christian life as life "in Christ," and this can best be understood as life in a field of force generated by Jesus' life, death, and resurrection. The compilers of Q and the Gospel writers who used Q were impressed by the power of Jesus' teaching. Both the field of force and encounter with the teaching of Jesus open believers to the effective work of creative transformation.

The idea of a field of force is not a mysterious one from Whitehead's point of view. Every event pervades its future. Of course, the effect of most of these events, including human ones, in the future they pervade is negligible. But there are important events as well, whose field of force is not negligible. The life of Jesus was an important event, and its repeated reenactment and remembrance has strengthened its field of force.

To be in a field of force is to conform in some measure with the event that generates the field. Thus to be in Paul's sense "in Christ" is to conform in some measure to Jesus. Since Jesus was himself open to creative transformation, to conform to him is to share in that openness.

Genuinely to hear Jesus' teaching is also to be opened to Christ as creative transformation. Whitehead noted how that teaching, just because of its impracticality and purity, creates restlessness with every existing system. When the world one is inclined to take for granted is rendered questionable, one is open to creative transformation.

Jesus also speaks directly to the hearers of their own existence. In the words of Reinhold Niebuhr, he afflicts the comfortable and comforts the afflicted. He makes our virtue questionable and assures us in our sinfulness. By reversing our self-evaluation he opens us to creative transformation.

That Jesus' work in so many ways opens believers to Christ as creative transformation justifies the close association of creative transformation with him. It also raises the question of how creative transformation was at work in him. In other words, how was God related to him? What was the structure of his own existence? Was he in this respect a Jewish prophet, a Christian, or something else?

All efforts to describe the structure of existence of an individual

or a community are speculative inferences from their writings or
their work. They do not intend to describe a fixed and given structure that characterizes people constantly while waking and sleep-
ing from birth to death. The effort is to describe that structure of
existence which underlies the distinctive work or especially remarkable characteristics of people. In Jesus' case, this can only
mean that we attempt to describe the structure of existence which
comes to expression in his authentic sayings.

Two characteristics of these sayings are noteworthy in this connection. First, the sayings express a peculiarly immediate and un-
distorted insight into life. Second, Jesus spoke, and otherwise
acted, as if he regarded himself as having peculiar authority. The
implicit claim to authority went beyond that of the prophets and
contrasted with believers' sense of dependence upon him. Jesus'
structure of existence seems to have been distinctive, and the distinctiveness seems to have centered in the mode of its relation to
God.

In this respect, we are at one with traditional Christologies.
However, their description of the distinctiveness of God's presence
in Jesus entailed the denial of the full humanity of Jesus. This was
due in part to substance metaphysics, which required that, if the
divine Logos were present in Jesus, then some part of his human
nature had to be displaced. It was also due in part to the desire to
support claims about Jesus' infallibility—only if God's relation to
Jesus were totally different from God's relation to others, so that
Jesus' speaking was really God's, could one accept Jesus' message
as the authoritative word of God. For us, Jesus' relation to God
can involve no denial of his full humanity. We have already seen
that process thought provides the basis for holding both of these
ideas together. Every actuality is an occasion of experience, in
which other experiences, including the divine one, are incarnated.
Hence there is no need for displacement, and the presence of God
in Jesus does not make Jesus an exception to actuality in general,
let alone humanity. What is necessary, within this context, is a way
of thinking of how Jesus' relation to God could be distinctive in
such a way as to account for the special characteristics of his
sayings.

One way in which structures of existence are differentiated is according to the constitution of the integrating center of experience, the self or the "I." In our infancy this organizing center is controlled largely by bodily events, but in our adult experience it is normally constituted by the effective presence of our own personal past. Our experience is organized in terms of purposes and memories inherited from our past. This route of inheritance determines our sense of self-identity through time.

There is, however, in all our experience also the divine presence and agency, the initial aim, the principle of creative transformation. This aim is at what would be best in each moment in terms of a wider view of the consequences than we ordinarily take. There is a tension between oneself and one's experience of what ideally would be, between what one is and the rightness in things that one dimly discerns. Hence the divine presence is experienced as an other, sometimes recognized as gracious, often felt as judge.

In Jesus' authentic sayings an existence expresses itself which does not experience this otherness of the divine. Instead, his selfhood seems to be constituted as much by the divine agency within him as by his own personal past. We may think of Jesus' structure of existence in terms of an "I" that is co-constituted by its inheritance from its personal past and by the initial aims derived from God. There is not the normal tension between the initial aims and the purposes received from the past, in that those past purposes were themselves conformed to divine aims and thereby involved the basic disposition to be open to God's call in each future moment. Whereas Christ is incarnate in everyone, Jesus *is* Christ because the incarnation is constitutive of his very selfhood. The affinities of this view with the Chalcedonian creed do not prove its truth, but if we take seriously the theological motivations that led to that creed, they give added reason for interest.

Although Christ works in us regardless of what we think about the exact nature of Christ's presence in Jesus, the question of the structure of Jesus' existence is not merely idle speculation. The work of Christ in us is enhanced as we accept Jesus as God's decisive revelation, and hence think of God as creative-responsive love. It is also enhanced as we deliberately place ourselves in his field of force, and as we renew our contact with his teaching. As we do these things, we allow our mode of existence to be decisively shaped by him. The extent to which we thus open ourselves to him is guided by our sense of his authority. In the past this authority was based on supernaturalist views. Today we believe that Jesus was in every sense fully human. But if we stop with that, we are in danger of losing the reason for our special attention to him. We need to clarify how, as a fully human person, Jesus could nevertheless speak and act in God's behalf and address us, even today, with authority. It is difficult to believe that God actually was decisively revealed through Jesus unless we have some notion as to how this was possible. We can understand these things best if we are led by the evidence to attribute to him a distinctive structure of existence such as that proposed above. This distinctiveness involves no violation of general principles, but is one more example of discontinuity within continuity.

THE CHURCH AS
THE BODY OF CHRIST

Christ has been defined as the Logos incarnate which operates as creative transformation. Christ in this sense can be found in all things and especially wherever there is life. The marks of his work are particularly manifest among human beings who are capable of incarnating in a heightened manner the novelty that marks his presence. Among human beings Christ's effectiveness is especially present where people open themselves to him. Such openness is facilitated where Christ is rightly named. It is facilitated also where the relation to Jesus shatters our pretenses and assures us in our brokenness.

The relation to Jesus that facilitates the work of Christ is maintained consciously and intentionally, especially through the proclamation of the word and the participation in the sacraments. These are marks of the church, and wherever authentic word and sacrament are present there is the church. But the reality of the church is deeper than is sometimes understood when this definition is employed; for in the community of the church sustained through word and sacrament Jesus himself is present to the believer. This presence constitutes the church as the Body of Christ and as the extension of that incarnation which was begun in Jesus. This is language that has been in tension with the dominant modern conceptuality, and hence the intuitions that it expresses have been largely suppressed in favor of purely psychological and sociological accounts. But Whitehead provides us with an avenue for deepening psychology and sociology once more into ontology and metaphysics. He enables us to understand that Jesus is really present in his church and that it is unity with him that constitutes membership in the church.

The preceding section approached this theme through mention of Paul's understanding of being "in Christ." This meant that the believer entered into the sphere of Jesus' influence and in that sphere conformed in some measure to him. This is correct, but it does not yet suggest the full sense of the real presence of Jesus. When Whitehead speaks of an event as pervading its future, he means that the event literally plays a constitutive role in the events that lie in its future. It is really present in each of these events. Subsequent events do not choose whether or not to be partly constituted by this event. They decide only *how* to take account of it. How a successor incorporates its predecessor affects the potency of that predecessor in still later events. Since in most cases the decision progressively weakens the predecessor's effect, most fields of force peter out quickly, as far as significant influence is concerned. But throughout its field of force an event plays some role in constituting all others.

In the case of Jesus we have to do not only with an event of great intrinsic power but also with one that has produced the church which accepts as its task the amplification of the field of force. Millions of persons have made decisions to be constituted by the event of Jesus in such a way that its potential for constituting others is increased. These decisions have shaped sacraments, whose purpose it is to re-present the events for enhanced efficacy in the lives of believers. Thus the church is the community that is consciously dedicated to maintaining, extending, and strengthening the field of force generated by Jesus. To enter such a community is to be engrafted into that field of force and thus to experience the real presence of Jesus constituting one's own existence.

The image of a field of force is not different from what Paul meant by the body of Christ. To be in Christ is to be a part of a body that is constituted by the real presence in the believers of the life, death, and resurrection of Jesus. The results are, therefore, not to be understood psychologically alone as the consequences of the attitudes adopted or sociologically alone as the consequences of the association with other believers. They are to be understood as the real efficacy of Jesus Christ as this is enhanced and intensified by suitable psychological and sociological factors.

THE TRINITY

In the early church, Christology and the formulation of Trinitarian doctrine went hand in hand. The process Christology described in this chapter gives rise to many of the same questions as did the Patristic discussion. It is fitting, therefore, to introduce a brief discussion of the Trinity into this chapter on process Christology.

The fundamental issue debated in the early church was the question of the relation of the divine that was incarnate in Jesus to deity itself. Was deity itself so radically transcendent that it was blasphemous, as Arius thought, to speak of God as incarnate in a mortal? In this case the divine reality that was present in Jesus must be creaturely, as Arius taught, or a subordinate and derivative aspect of deity, as many of the Origenists supposed. Under the leadership of Athanasius the church came finally to insist that, although one could distinguish the divine that was incarnate in Jesus from other aspects of deity, it was coequal with those other aspects and participated equally with them in deity itself. It was deity itself that was incarnate in Jesus.

In the formulation of process Christology proposed above, the Athanasian conclusion follows. God as creative love, the Primordial Nature of God, is what is incarnate in Jesus. This is not a creature of God or a derivative and subordinate aspect of deity. It is distinguishable from other aspects of deity, but it is coequal with them and participates equally with them in deity itself. God as incarnate in the world is not inferior to God as transcending the world. It was deity itself that was incarnate in Jesus. It is as true to say that God transcendent is abstracted from God immanent as to say that God immanent is abstracted from God transcendent. There is only one deity which by its very nature is both immanent and transcendent.

The early church decided that there was a second, distinguishable way in which God was immanent in the world. This was the Holy Spirit. The church believed that the distinction was not only in the human mode of experiencing the divine but in the divine life itself. It concluded that in this instance, too, the divine reality that is present as Holy Spirit is fully God.

With these conclusions process theology can also agree. In addition to the presence in the world of the creative love of God (the Primordial Nature), there is also the presence of the responsive love of God (the Consequent Nature). The responsive love of God is just as fully God as is the creative love of God.

These are the fundamental Christian affirmations from which the doctrine of the Trinity has been fashioned, and process theology affirms and clarifies them. Yet this clarification leads to tensions with traditional formulations of the Trinitarian dogma, for it does not lead to a view of three aspects of God that are persons in the same sense. When "person" is taken in its modern sense, God is one person. When "person" is taken in its traditional sense, two persons can be distinguished, God as creative love and God as responsive love. Both these persons have a transcendent and an immanent aspect, and therefore if we add this distinction to the one between the persons we have a quaternity. If instead we add to the thought of the two persons the unity in which they are held together in the one God, then we have a trinity, but the unity is not another person in the same sense that the other two are persons.

The doctrine of the Trinity is the heart of Christian faith, a source of distortion, and an artificial game that has brought theology into justifiable disrepute. It is the heart of faith insofar as Christians believe that the one God is truly present to them for their salvation in Jesus Christ and in the Holy Spirit. This is crucial, since it lies behind the conviction that what was manifest in Jesus, i.e., creative-responsive love, is the basic reality in the universe and hence that with which we want to align ourselves, and that this sacred reality can be experienced in our present mode of existence.

The doctrine of the Trinity is a source of distortion in Christian faith insofar as it has suggested that the most divine aspect of God is other than that which was manifest in Jesus. Although the decisions at Nicaea and Constantinople said that all three "persons" were equally divine, the feeling remained that God the Father was more ultimately God than the other two persons. Hence the feeling was supported that the essence of deity is something other than creative-responsive love. Theologians even developed technical terms that explicitly stated this point, such as the distinction between God's "revealed will" and his "hidden will"—and the world was said finally to be ruled by the latter. Hence, partly due to the insistence upon three persons, the formal confession that Jesus was the decisive revelation of God was thereby not allowed to revolutionize the conception of deity.

The doctrine of the Trinity is an artificial game when much ado is made of the number three, and when the "mystery" that God is somehow three in one is portrayed as of special significance in itself, and even as central to Christian faith. Discussions of the various aspects of deity are meaningful only insofar as they help clarify experience in general and Christian experience in particular. Hence process theology is not interested in formulating distinctions within God for the sake of conforming with traditional Trinitarian notions. As with other doctrines, we find that there is helpful guidance in the traditional doctrine and much with which to agree in basic intention, but that the previous formulation is in need of modification. We have suggested that the main distinction to be made is that between the creative and responsive sides of the divine love.

7

ESCHATOLOGY

THE FUTURE OF HISTORY

Teilhard de Chardin wrote: "Although we too often forget this, what we call evolution develops only in virtue of a certain internal preference for survival (or, if you prefer to put it so, self-survival) which in man takes on a markedly psychic appearance, in the form of a *zest for life*. Ultimately, it is that and that alone which underlies and supports the whole complex of biophysical energies whose operation, acting experimentally, conditions anthropogenesis.

"In view of that fact, what would happen if one day we should see that the universe is so hermetically closed in upon itself that there is no possible way of our emerging from it—either because we are forced indefinitely to go round and round inside it, or (which comes to the same thing) because we are doomed to a total death? Immediately and without further ado, I believe—just like miners who find that the gallery is blocked ahead of them—we would lose the heart to act, and man's impetus would be radically checked and 'deflated' for ever, by this fundamental discouragement and *loss of zest.*" (Teilhard de Chardin, *Science and Christ,* tr. by René Hague [Harper & Row, Publishers, Inc., 1968], pp. 212–213.)

Teilhard here powerfully puts before us the importance of hope. Whitehead also knew that zest was lost where there was no vision of new perfections to be attained. Precisely now, when the future of Western humanistic civilization and indeed the global future appear so bleak, the Christian message of hope becomes particularly important.

Whitehead provides grounds for hope for history. First, the future is fully and radically open. It must take account of all that has been, but the past never settles just how the future will take account of it. Its freedom in relation to the present is not merely that it can readjust the elements in the present world with differing emphases. It can also introduce wholly new elements that change the weight and meaning of those it inherits from the present. Hence projections of the future are never more than warnings of what will be if . . . , that is, if they are not heeded, if they do not prompt new thinking and new deeds.

Second, Whitehead believes that progress can occur. New ideals can enter history and slowly produce changes that make their embodiment possible. The ideals of Jesus' message have brought us in the direction of their practicability. They can carry us farther. Institutions can be changed by ideas as well as by force. The changes can be for the better.

The conviction that the future is open and that progress is possible is even more important now than when Whitehead wrote, but it does not suffice. The degree of alienation from ordinary historical processes is such that their gradual melioration does not inspire the zest of which Teilhard wrote. Without the zest, even that melioration is not likely to occur. Teilhard's vision of a much more radical change, though less "realistic" and "probable," has more capacity to produce the will to survive apart from which survival itself is threatened. Its limitation, on the other hand, is that Omega seems so remote from us that it seems to many more like a dream or wishful thinking than a real hope. We need some intermediate forms of hope more radical than the melioration of our present problems but more proximate than an ultimate consummation in Omega. Whitehead can help us here in ways that point in the same direction as Teilhard.

The hope we need is for a radical change in the very quality of our existence. We have broken out of the villages and urban neighborhoods where community is established by our familial connections and our assigned roles. This break has been partly caused by an inner dynamic in technology and economics that is not of our choosing, and partly caused by our finding those "natural" communities oppressive. To become free individuals we gave up the emotional and personal security of such given community with its provision to each of us of a settled place. Increasingly we are giving up even the nuclear family. We do not want to return, but we find our supposed freedom illusory. We are free to do what we want, but we do not want anything very much. Further, our freedom is bought at the price of isolation and loneliness. Because we cannot exist without interdependence, we call on governments to mediate between us. But governments are impersonal and remote. Our freedom from persons with whom we had rich mutual relations is transformed into bondage to an impersonal system.

When we were caught in the bondage of natural communities, we developed a vision of personal freedom. That vision gave us zest and purpose. But now that we experience that freedom as loneliness and dependence on impersonal institutions, we lack a vision of what can free us and fulfill us. Hence, there is a loss of zest and a dangerous tolerance of controls from social systems, controls that we do not tolerate from personal communities.

The vision that is needed is of new communities that are not experienced as restrictive of freedom. They must be voluntary communities, but that is not enough. Voluntarily to accept the oppression that was felt in involuntary communities is not improvement. But a contractual community is not adequate either. Contracts may be needed among individuals who remain essentially isolated individuals, and these contracts may be better than the restrictions imposed by natural communities, but they too are oppressive. The voluntary community must be bound by different kinds of ties, ties that are experienced as fulfillment rather than limitation.

This is an appropriate vision for Christians, since in its origin the church was this kind of community. It was not without its problems, of course, but it was a voluntary community in which interpersonal relations were experienced chiefly as liberating rather than restricting. People could think of themselves as members one of the other in the intimate way in which the parts of the body belong to one another. For brief periods sectarian and monastic groups have recovered this sense of new community, but on the whole it has been lost to the churches. The ideal of inclusive membership has reduced the voluntary element and made of the church another natural community. Where the element of the voluntary has remained, the church has usually been more a group of individuals with contractual relations than a new community of love.

The lesson often taken from this is that a voluntary community of mutual participation is historically possible only under special circumstances and inevitably decays rapidly into a natural or contractual one. There are other, more hopeful, interpretations. The original small voluntary communities grew larger and eventually became all-inclusive in large geographical areas. The church continued to expand through the nineteenth century. During this expansion, despite exceptions, it lost its original voluntary and intimate character. Participation in a church, as in a village or nation, became chiefly a matter of birth and location. That is, the church became a "natural" community. But it nevertheless encouraged the ideal of individual freedom. This ideal broke through the natural community and either led to the abandonment of the church altogether or created new contractual institutions. Even where the church still operates by the ideal of the natural community, it is being forced away from such community by world history and by the individualism it has fostered. Also, in the twentieth century it has ceased to expand. It has become global, but in the process it has discovered other traditions over which it cannot desire to be simply victorious. It has adopted pluralism. These factors mean that, having become global, it is now forced back upon its interior life as a voluntary community, dissatisfied with merely contractual arrangements and remembering an original community of mutual participation. If that dim dream becomes a vivid desire, the church could move into a new era.

One obstacle to the transformation of the dream into a purpose is conceptual. To aim seriously at something we must suppose that it is possible and have sufficient clarity as to what is aimed at to see in outline how it could occur. Our dominant conceptualities do not allow this. We perceive the given reality to be the individual psychophysical person, bounded by her or his skin. Each person remains external to all others. In this view, even sexual union is union only in name, for it cannot involve more than extended external contact. In short, all relations are viewed as external. One person does things to another and receives the effects of the actions of the other.

If this were the ontological reality, then talk of being members one of another would be a misleading image referring at most to certain emotions of intimacy. But according to Teilhard and to Whitehead this is not the reality. Whitehead, using the term "body" in its conventional sense, states that it is merely the most intimate part of the environment. (*PR* 126.) The whole world is the environment. Teilhard, with the same insight, speaks with a more striking rhetoric. "Hitherto, the prevailing view has been that the body (that is to say, the matter that is *incommunicably* attached to each soul) is a *fragment* of the universe—a piece *completely detached* from the rest and handed over to a spirit that informs it. In future, we shall say that the Body is the very Universality of things, in as much as they are centred on an animating Spirit, in as much as they influence that Spirit—and are themselves influenced and sustained by it. . . . My own body is not these cells or those cells that *belong exclusively* to me: it is *what*, in these cells *and* in the rest of the world, feels my influence and reacts against me. *My* matter is not a *part* of the universe that I possess *totaliter:* it is the *totality* of the Universe possessed by me *partialiter.*" (Teilhard de Chardin, *Science and Christ*, pp. 12–13.)

This is a very different vision from the one of separate psycho-physical persons communicating with one another only externally. It means that in fact we are parts of one another's bodies. That is an idea that *could* have profound effects as it adventures through history. Whether we must wait for centuries before this idea can overcome the existential effects of the idea of mutually external individuals, with which we have lived so long, remains to be seen. But we can hope that its existential realization will come sooner. That would mean that the idea of mutual participation would bring into prominence in our experience the already existing fact (which we know at the prethematic level) of mutual participation, and that this would change the nature and direction of our basic purposes. The actual character of our self-identity through time would be altered. We would enter into a new structure of existence that would ground in an enduring way the community that was temporarily realized as a promise in the early church.

In some respects, however, the community toward which this understanding points would be different from the early Christian one. That one was restricted in two ways. First, a sharp line was drawn between believers and nonbelievers. Second, the intensity of the mutual participation between human beings separated the Christians farther from nature, including their own bodies, than had been the case in either Judaism or Hellenism. This double limitation was no doubt necessary at that time to the achievement of communities of mutual participation.

Teilhard, however, asserts that the universe is my body. Whitehead says, "The actual world is mine." (*PR* 117.) In that case the Christian communities for which we may hope would still be only the most immediate part of the environment. The environment that is the true body would extend beyond it to all human beings and to all creatures. The sense of mutual participation with all life and even with the inanimate world would radically alter the way we treat the environment. We would realize with Whitehead that all "life is robbery" and that "the robber requires justification." (*PR* 160.) There are reasons to *use* our bodies even when damage is involved, but there is never any justification for reckless abuse. When we have existentially realized that we are continuous with the environment, that the environment is our body, then we will find new styles of life appropriate to that realization.

This vision will also change our relations to our bodies in the ordinary sense. For a long time our concepts have juxtaposed our souls or minds to our bodies. The body has thus been alien to our true selves as well as to the bodies of others. As a result we have viewed our bodies as something to use or control. In reaction against such a view there has been in recent literature an insistence that we *are* our bodies. This opens to us the possibility of the immediate enjoyment of bodily feelings which we have repressed, and it counters false tendencies to view ourselves as purely spiritual or transcendent beings. But if taken with full seriousness, it would destroy the tendency to prize freedom and equality which had its origin in the doctrine of the immeasurable worth of the human soul independent of the health or beauty of the body. It would also leave the individual bodies mutually external and alien.

Whitehead's vision of the body as the more intimate part of the environment preserves the distinctness of the soul while destroying its separation from the body. The occasions of the soul's life are constituted by the presence in it of the environment. These soul occasions are indeed nothing but the peculiarly rich prehensive unifications of the universe made possible by the extraordinary construction of the body. It is indeed bodily feelings that are dominantly constitutive of the soul's experience. Our failure to appreciate this is caused by the peculiarity of consciousness in highlighting that aspect of the soul's experience which is originated in the soul. The massive sense of inheritance from the body is overlaid in consciousness by sense perception, in which the sense of derivation from the body is largely lost; and even the perception of the body is primarily an external one. Maurice Merleau-Ponty's phenomenological analysis of the experience of the body helps to overcome this fallacy of misplaced concreteness. Whitehead's conceptuality can carry this task farther.

This is a vision of a possible future. Radical changes in human self-understanding are possible, accompanied by actual changes in the structure of existence. The structure called for is the one that would most fully adapt human existence to the ontological reality that is already given, and that we already know at the prethematized level of our experience. There are forces already discernible driving us toward this ideal and toward its realization. Nevertheless, the Whiteheadian, unlike Teilhard, must assert that in this respect, too, the future is open. There is no assurance that the human species will move forward. It cannot stand still, but in the face of its massive dangers it may decay or even destroy itself. Even if this new level of human existence were attained, and other levels beyond it, there would be no End at which the process would come to rest. This means that the problem of evil is not solved by images of historical hope.

THE KINGDOM OF HEAVEN

The theoretical problem of evil has been treated at some length in Chapters 3 and 4. But it has another side. The problem is not only the theoretical one of God's responsibility for evil, it is also a practical and existential one. Evil is experienced as an overwhelming destructive power against which we find ourselves quite helpless. Merely to see that the existence of a good God is compatible with evil does not suffice. Our concern is also that this evil be overcome or at least that we be assured that evil does not have the last word.

A major reason that Christian theism has clung so long to notions of God as Controlling Power is that thereby it can assure believers that God's will, despite all appearances, is victorious. For the sake of this assurance it has risked seeing God as the author of needless suffering and even moral evil. It has risked the implicit denial of human freedom and the rebellion of humanistic atheism.

Process theism does not take these risks and accordingly cannot provide the assurance that God's will is always done. It does affirm that, no matter how great the evil in the world, God acts persuasively upon the wreckage to bring from it whatever good is possible. It asserts that this persuasive power with its infinite persistence is in fact the greatest of all powers. But it does not find in that assertion assurance that any particular evil, including the evil of the imminent self-destruction of the human race, can be ruled out. God persuades against it, but there is no guarantee that we will give heed. God does not act *ex machina* to prevent the consequences of destructive human acts. Critics object that a being not able to guarantee a favorable outcome to the process does not have the sort of power that is essential to deity. On this ground process theology is accused of atheism.

At this point process theology does side with the atheist against the traditional theist. It does insist that the future is truly open and that what will happen depends upon what human beings will do.

But whereas atheists see the power of human beings to shape their own destiny as arising out of their own given being or out of antecedent nature, process theology sees it as arising out of the persuasive power of God. It is because God exercises power upon us, persuasive power, that a space is opened up for us within which we are free. If there were no God, there would be no freedom, and the future would not be open to be shaped by human decision. The future is open and we are free because of God. The power to open the future and give us freedom is a greater power than the supposed power of absolute control, for a power effective over free beings is a far greater power than what would be involved in the manipulation of robots.

Clearly, therefore, the charge of atheism is misplaced, unless "theism" is narrowly defined. But the problem of evil remains, not only as a challenge to our thought and stamina but also as a threat to the will to live and serve. A being who does not overcome this final threat of evil cannot be worshiped as God.

This does not mean that God must prevent everything we regard as evil. Traditional theism has never supposed that, for it is obvious that no God of that sort exists. Much that we regard as evil is not genuinely so. We complain about our poverty or our failure to succeed in competition, whereas with spiritual maturity we can sometimes discover either that our poverty and failure have enriched our lives or that they have driven us to seek more important goods. What seems evil but ceases to be so when the Christian transvaluation of values occurs is not the evil that God must overcome in order to be worshiped as God.

Further, as Chapter 4 showed, there is much evil that is made possible by the risk taken by divine creative love in order to overcome triviality. The possibility of this sin and suffering is necessarily entailed in the creation of beings capable of high grades of enjoyment. God neither prevents this evil, nor guarantees compensation for it, although the divine creative love does encourage us to avoid unnecessary discord and to transform situations creatively so as to bring good out of evil. Rebelling against the universe because of this kind of evil reflects a misunderstanding not only of what perfect power can and cannot do, but also of the nature of evil, i.e., of the fact that triviality is as much to be avoided as discord.

But there is a deeper evil, and the longing that this evil not have the last word is not based upon immature desires or inadequate understandings of the nature of things. The deepest problem is not finally injustice, physical suffering, or mental anguish. That they are pervasive of the world is beyond question, but in spite of them there is an enjoyment of life such that we can find meaning in caring about all things, and such that for the sake of life we can try to mitigate injustice and to reduce suffering and anguish. The final problem is not death, for even untimely death need not destroy the meaning and worth of the life that has been lived. The deepest problem is temporality as such, which Whitehead, borrowing a phrase from Locke, calls perpetual perishing. "The ultimate evil in the temporal world is deeper than any specific evil. It lies in the fact that the past fades, that time is a 'perpetual perishing.' " (*PR* 517.) What destroys in our maturity the zest of our youth is not so much the discovery that injustice, suffering, and anguish are a part of all life; it is the realization that the moments of joy in which these evils are overcome fade into dim memories and are finally lost altogether. The conviction that success does not ultimately succeed undercuts our zest more radically than do many failures.

If this perpetual perishing of everything that we value is the whole story, then life is ultimately meaningless. Although there is enjoyment and hence intrinsic value in every present experience, in and for itself, conscious reflection upon the fact that everything we accomplish and enjoy will pass into oblivion can undercut the value of this immediate enjoyment. In this light, the emergence of beings with the capacity for conscious reflection about ultimate meaning would be a great evil, for the greater enjoyment that this high level of consciousness makes possible would be destroyed by this consciousness itself.

The desire that this ultimate evil be overcome is part of that love for all things toward which we are lured by God. If the last word is perishing, then the call to love all things cannot be part of a message of good news. With the conviction that the existence of all things is ultimately futile, that their triumphs are finally meaningless, love for them would heighten suffering to a humanly unendurable point. We would have to recognize the superior wisdom of those in the West who have seen happiness only in apathy and those in the East who have called for cessation of desire in perfect detachment. The possibility of Christian caring is bound up with the assurance that the one who gives us the spirit of caring also provides for the deepest needs of those for whom we care.

The fact that the structure of temporality as perpetual perishing is for us the final evil is rooted in the basic ontological drive toward self-expression, which is rooted in turn in the divine aim not only to achieve enjoyment in the immediate present but also to contribute value to the future. We want to have instrumental as well as intrinsic value. Anticipating that our experiences will be instrumentally valuable means believing them to be meaningful. For beings with the power of reflection, this sense of meaningfulness is necessary if even the positive intrinsic value of the present is to be retained. Furthermore, the instrumental value of our lives cannot be of limited duration. As Whitehead says: "Conscious, rational life refuses to conceive itself as a transient enjoyment, transiently useful." (*PR* 516.)

Traditional theology has dealt with the evil involved in temporality by contrasting God's eternity with our temporality. But this is exactly the wrong solution. Whitehead wrote: "So long as the temporal world is conceived as a self-sufficient completion of the creative act, explicable by its derivation from an ultimate principle which is at once ultimately real and the unmoved mover, from this conclusion there is no escape: the best that we can say of the turmoil is, 'For so he giveth his beloved—sleep.'" (*PR* 519.) Whitehead's point is that in such a vision we can contribute nothing to God, the converse of which is that God cannot save our experiences from final meaninglessness. The most that would be possible would be endless ongoingness. But endless ongoingness would only protract forever the perpetual perishing that is the ultimate evil. This has been fully realized in India, and as a result much Indian religion has sought release in Nirvana.

But if God is responsive love, our basic situation is quite different. If God is responsive to us, then our joys and deeds affect deity itself. However rapidly their worldly effects fade in the course of time, their importance is established in that they have mattered in the divine life. This divine life is neither eternal, in the sense of timeless, nor temporal, in the sense of perpetual perishing. Instead it is everlasting, constantly receiving from the world but retaining what in the world is past in the immediacy of its everlasting present. Whitehead saw that " 'everlastingness' is the content of that vision upon which the finer religions are built—the 'many' absorbed everlastingly in the final unity." (*PR* 527.)

This everlasting reality is the kingdom of heaven. The kingdom of heaven is "the temporal world perfected by its reception and reformation as a fulfillment of the primordial appetite which is the basis of all order." (*PR* 507.) Human life finds its special *raison d'être* within this vision. For it is capable of "the more distinctly human experiences of beauty," as well as truth and morality; and "all three types of character partake in the highest ideal of satisfaction possible for actual realization, and in this sense can be termed that final beauty which provides the final contentment for the Eros of the Universe." (*AI* 13.) Furthermore, all the other things for which we are called to care have their ultimate meaning grounded in God's responsive love. God's Consequent Nature is not exclusive. It "prehends every actuality for what it can be in such a perfected system—its suffering, its sorrows, its failures, its triumphs, its immediacies of joy—woven by rightness of feeling into the harmony of universal feeling, which is always immediate, always many, always one, always with novel advance, moving onward and never perishing. The revolts of destructive evil, purely self-regarding, are dismissed into their triviality of merely individual facts; and yet the good they did achieve in individual joy, in individual sorrow, in the introduction of needed contrast, is yet saved by its relation to the completed whole. The image—and it is but an image—the image under which this operative growth of God's nature is best conceived, is that of a tender care that nothing be lost." (*PR* 525.)

Philosophically Whitehead's images raise problems of interpretation that are still under discussion. He himself distinguished between the intuition of the basic point and the possibility of conceptualizing it: "This immortality of the World of Action, derived from its transformation in God's nature, is beyond our imagination to conceive. The various attempts at description are often shocking and profane. What does haunt our imagination is that the immediate facts of present action pass into permanent significance for the Universe." (*Imm.* 698.)

Thus the basic point is clear. It is Whitehead's explanation of his statement that, although process entails loss in the temporal world, "there is no reason, of any ultimate metaphysical generality, why this should be the whole story." (*PR* 517.) God's responsive love is the power to overcome the final evil of our temporal existence. Because of God, life has meaning in the face of victorious evil. That meaning is that both in our own enjoyment and through our adding to the enjoyment of others we contribute everlastingly to the joy of God. That meaning is simultaneously that we are always safe with God.

Some process theologians have believed that, though perpetual perishing is a more ultimate evil than death, personal death is also so fundamental that we must ask how God overcomes this evil as well. They have considered the possibility of renewed personal existence after death as contributing to the solution of this problem, and they have found that Whitehead's conceptuality allows for such views even if he himself did not adopt them. He himself said that his philosophy is "entirely neutral on the question of immortality." (*RM* 107.) On the one hand, it gives no warrant for the belief that the human soul is necessarily immortal. *(Ibid.)* On the other hand, by its clear distinction of the soul from the body and its clarification of possible relations not mediated by bodies, it leaves open the possibility that the soul may live again after death: "In some important sense the existence of the soul may be freed from its complete dependence upon the bodily organization." (*AI* 267.) Whitehead writes that "there is no reason why such a question should not be decided on more special evidence." (*RM* 111.) Some Christians believe that such evidence is provided in the resurrection of Jesus, and if so, process theology is open to affirming personal life after death. But such an idea is difficult to formulate in a way that is not "shocking and profane."

Whitehead was sensitive to the concern for the preservation of persons as well as events. His image of everlastingness in God was fashioned with personal existence in view. He wrote: "An enduring personality in the temporal world is a route of occasions in which the successors with some peculiar completeness sum up their predecessors. The correlate fact in God's nature is an even more complete unity of life in a chain of elements for which succession does not mean loss of immediate unison. This element in God's nature inherits from the temporal counterpart according to the same principle as that by which in the temporal world the future inherits from the past. Thus in the sense in which the present occasion is the person *now*, and yet with his own past, so the counterpart in God is that person in God." (*PR* 531–532.)

The expression of Christian eschatology in Whiteheadian terms is still in process. There is agreement that human life is something more than a succession of events between birth and death, that God aims at personal life as the condition of intensities of experience, that God saves what can be saved. There is assurance that death and perpetual perishing are not the last word. But there remains a profound mystery which even Whitehead's intuition could not penetrate.

PEACE

In addition to opening up the imagination for new possibilities to be realized in the historical future, and assuring us that whatever happens our actions are cherished in God, Whitehead speaks of the spiritual consummation of our lives here and now. He calls this "Peace." It is a special factor in an occasion's enjoyment, and it is bound in a special way to the occasion's relation to God.

Enjoyment characterizes experiences in their individuality insofar as they attain some measure of harmony and intensity of feeling. But the attainment of enjoyment by one occasion may reduce the enjoyment possible for others, and enjoyment now may be at the expense of enjoyment later within the same enduring individual. Awareness of these tensions inhibits enjoyment in the present.

What is needed is a larger harmony, what Whitehead calls a "Harmony of Harmonies" that can exclude "the restless egotism" with which enjoyment is often pursued. (*AI* 367.) When this occurs it is through the relation to God.

It is first of all through the relation to the Primordial Nature of God. God has an aim for every experience that is in some measure felt conformally in that experience. The aim persuasively acts within that experience, but the experience makes its own decision in terms of the multiplicity of inherited interests. For example, a human being is influenced by hopes and fears derived from past moments of life as well as by the aim derived from God. If that aim calls for an action that is anticipated with fear, it may well be refused. More generally, there is a tension between the tendency to narrow self-interest and God's aim for a self-actualization that conduces also to the wider good.

Although the initial aim derived from God is not perfectly fulfilled, it is not ineffective. Because of God's presence in us in this form, "our purposes extend beyond values for ourselves to values for others." (*RM* 152.) Because of God we experience unrealized ideals; and adventure, morality, and religion all result from this. We are dimly aware of a rightness in things "attained or missed, with more or less completeness of attainment or omission." (*RM* 60–61.) But we have seen that this rightness does not lend itself to a single formulation of the right way to live or act. What is right for one occasion is not right for another. Indeed the aim for each occasion differs.

As long as we try to solve the problems that ensue through our rational and calculative procedures, tensions remain, for we cannot calculate the relative importance of morality and adventure, and there is no assurance that the results of our best calculations will coincide with God's aim. God's aim is in terms of the inclusive reality beyond the possibility of our minds to fathom. It is for that outcome which is the best in this situation. To whatever extent our lives become aligned to God's ever-changing aims for us, we can have "that Peace, which is the harmony of the soul's activities with ideal aims that lie beyond any personal satisfaction." (*AI* 371.)

Whitehead does not propose a method for attaining peace. He

notes that "the deliberate aim at Peace very easily passes into its
bastard substitute, Anaesthesia." (*AI* 368.) Instead of achieving a
harmony of rich harmonies, we are too likely to avoid the discords
apart from which strength of beauty is not attained. "The experience of Peace is largely beyond the control of purpose. It comes as
a gift." (*AI* 368.) It is the completion of the religious life.

Finally it is the immanence of deity as a whole, with its Primordial and Consequent Natures, its creative and responsive love,
which is the source of Peace: "It is the immanence of the Great
Fact including this initial Eros and this final Beauty which constitutes the zest of self-forgetful transcendence belonging to Civilization at its height. . . . The immediate experience of this Final Fact
. . . is the sense of Peace." (*AI* 381.) This Peace is "the removal
of the stress of acquisitive feeling arising from the soul's preoccupation with itself" and a consequent "surpassing of personality." (*AI*
367.) It is the surpassing of personality in which "the 'self' has been
lost, and interest has been transferred to coordinations wider than
personality." (*AI* 368.)

Process theologians find in Whitehead's analysis of the relation
of morality and Peace a contemporary rendering of the Christian
understanding of law and grace. Moral codes are of God in several
senses. First, there would be no morality at all except for the
distinction between possible ideals and actual things which God
introduces into the world. Second, these codes express the widen-
ing of concern that God specifically causes in us. Third, they are
necessary to sustain the forms of order that make possible the
individual realizations of enjoyment that are part of God's aim.
Thus the law is holy, just, and good. It is itself a gift of God. But
it does not have the power to save us. It often adds to the discord
within our experience. It can render us insensitive to new modes
of enjoyment struggling to be born. It can give us a false sense of
rightness that blinds us to the true rightness in things.

The presence of God in us is divine grace. (Cf. *AI* 205.) It gives
rise to adventure, and to art. To it we owe the beauty we experience
as well as the discord that makes us restless with the law. It works
at all times in all people. The supreme gift is Peace, which is an
alignment of ourselves with God's grace. This alignment occurs

only through our free decision to live from grace. This is perhaps why Whitehead says that "the experience of Peace is *largely* beyond the control of purpose." (*AI* 368; italics added.)

Grace frees us from the law in two senses. Peace fulfills the general intention of the law without opposing the requirements of the moral code to one's own interests. Peace also frees one to act differently from the way any moral code requires in the immediate enjoyment of beauty and in the voyage of adventure toward new forms of beauty. Most inclusively, Peace as an alignment with purposes derived from the divine wisdom allows one to act beyond all calculations of present and future beauty.

Peace does not do away with the general need for moral codes. Participation in Peace is at any rate a matter of degree. Moral codes are necessary training for those who do not yet enjoy Peace to a significant degree, and useful guides for all. But from the perspective of Peace they do not bind, and the note of obligation is removed.

In the body of Christ, where the words of Jesus are rightly heard, there is Peace. Peace is the gift of Christ and the fruit of the Spirit. Hence Peace is a mark of the church as the extension of the incarnation and the eschatological community. It characterizes Christian existence as that reflects the creative-responsive love of God. It is at once Christian freedom and Christian assurance.

8

❧❀❧

THE CHURCH IN
CREATIVE TRANSFORMATION

CHRIST AND THE CHURCHES

In Chapter 6 the church was described Christologically as the Body of Christ and the extension of the incarnation. In Chapter 7 it was seen as a voluntary community of mutual participation and as an eschatological community of Peace.

These statements about the church are intelligible in the categories of process theology. The problem with them is that they strain our credulity as we live in our empirical churches. What is the relation of the church for which these images have been used to the actual churches that are now extant? Is *the* church entirely past or entirely future? Or is it in some way the sum of all the present-day churches, or of some of them, or of some fragment of some of them? Is it in fact found more in the world outside the churches than within them? Is it possible, indeed, that the churches have closed themselves to Christ and so are not the church at all?

Ecclesiology today must concern itself as much with the relation of the extant churches to the church as with the shaping of ideal images of the church. In doing so it is forced to make a fundamental distinction. The normative images of the church include both the actual efficacy of Christ and the celebration and renewal of that efficacy through word and sacrament. Clearly these belong together. But in recent centuries we often discern the most striking efficacy of the power of creative transformation in the scientist, artist, and philosopher who stand outside the churches because they have rejected them or been rejected by them, or because they have been simply too bored by the churches to take them seriously.

Although the presence of Christ outside the churches is a judgment upon them, it does not render them superfluous. When movements stemming from Christ do not acknowledge him, they lose their commonality of purpose and issue in a fragmentation of activity and understanding that becomes dehumanizing. The modern university, into which so much of authentic Christian energy passes from the churches, all too clearly expresses this result. In the churches the true principle of unity and purpose is regularly acknowledged and reinforced, even when the implications of the action are truncated. In each generation much of the creative energy expressed outside the churches was originally generated within them. As long as the intention of obedience to Christ continues within the churches they provide the possibility of the reunion of form and substance in the normative church. And in some measure such union has always been present even in the fragmented churches.

One reason for the separation of the actual effective presence of Christ from the celebration of that presence in the churches is that the churches lost their nerve. In the face of the Protestant Reformation, the Counter-Reformation sought to save the church by preservation of past thought and practice. In the face of eighteenth-century rationalism and the dominance of the scientific mentality, Protestants followed suit. Of course the church had always intended to be faithful to its traditions, but throughout the early and medieval times this faithfulness was achieved by a dynamic process of rethinking the past in the light of current experience and of the best knowledge available. On the whole the most creative minds were the leading thinkers of the church. They did not experience the Christian faith as any more restrictive of their freedom to think honestly and openly than scientists today feel restricted by the methods and expectations of the scientific community. Similarly the Reformers found their new appreciation of Scripture liberating rather than restricting. It is only in more recent times that Christians have defined their beliefs in contradistinction to the most imaginative and critical thought of their day.

Whitehead shows that any movement must either advance or decay. There is no standing still. The effort to repeat the past while holding the present at bay leads to decadence. The vitality and zest that were of the essence of the worth of the past are lost. What remain are only dying forms. A movement "preserves its vigour so long as it harbours a real contrast between what has been and what may be, and so long as it is nerved by the vigour to adventure." (*AI* 360.) A living movement like a living person is continuously fashioning new syntheses of its own individual past and the new data with which external processes endlessly confront it.

As Roman Catholic and conservative Protestant churches relapsed into defense of their inheritance, the effort to deal responsibly with changing cultural and scientific advances was continued by liberal Protestants. Apart from their great theological achievements, Christian thought today could hardly survive outside of ghettos. Nevertheless, the overall course of liberal Protestantism has been a decline. During a period of unprecedented intellectual progress, each development "has found the religious thinkers unprepared. Something which has been proclaimed to be vital has finally, after struggle, distress, and anathema, been modified and otherwise interpreted. The next generation of religious apologists then congratulates the religious world on the deeper insight which has been gained." (*SMW* 270.) Through this process religious leaders have lost credibility, and "religion is tending to degenerate into a decent formula wherewith to embellish a comfortable life." (*SMW* 187.)

The retreat of liberal Christianity before advancing secular culture is expressed in talk about what we can "still" believe. Something is held on to as "still" compatible with modern knowledge. But this accommodation has the effect of what Whitehead calls anaesthesia. We achieve a harmony of selected elements of the inherited faith and of inescapable aspects of modernity by dulling the cutting edge of each. Whitehead's philosophy itself too often has been used by Christians to achieve some such low grade of harmony. Against the background of this trivialization, cries of traditionalists and anti-Christians ring with the potential of renewed intensity.

Whitehead points to another option for Christians. "A clash of doctrines is not a disaster—it is an opportunity. . . . Religion will not regain its old power until it can face change in the same spirit as does science." (*SMW* 266, 270.) Such a spirit can lead to deepened understanding and fresh insight, that is, to the creative transformation that is Christ. When Christians experience the clash of received doctrines, both with one another and with ideas coming from without, as an opportunity for purification, enrichment, deepening, and transformation of their heritage, they participate rightly in the church. To have faith is to trust Christ to transform us in unforeseeable ways rather than to predetermine what kinds of changes will be allowable. Pope John XXIII trusted Christ, and despite all hesitation and wavering, a new chapter in the history of the church is being written.

If the churches are to participate in *the* church, they must be creatively transformed through their openness to Christ. This means that they must accept ideas and practices against which they have been protecting themselves. But it does not mean that they should accept uncritically what is foreign to their traditions. Christ does not call us to *Kulturprotestantismus!* On the contrary, creative transformation for the Christian community involves the heightening of criticism both of itself and of that which it finds outside itself. It involves the critical appropriation of that which it discerns as the work of Christ in the world, at the price of whatever inner changes are thereby entailed. Such work is in fact now going on with impressive results. The catholic spirit is being released from its bondage in both Roman Catholicism and Protestantism.

Openness to Christ as creative transformation is rightly feared as a threat to the extant churches. The work of Christ they find outside themselves truly threatens them to the extent to which they have resisted Christ and thereby creative transformation. The Old Testament depicts Yahweh, the God acknowledged and celebrated in Israel, as using against Israel nations that did not acknowledge him. Similarly, Christ can work for the destruction of faithless churches through forces that deny him—and to some extent all churches are faithless. There is no assurance that as our extant churches open themselves to creative transformation they will survive as churches.

The churches confront two types of challenge. On the one side, there is the vast creativity of modern Western culture with its art, science, philosophy, historical scholarship, and movements for liberation. On the other side, there are the other great cultures and religious Ways of the world, with their profoundly different insights and ways of salvation. To give some concreteness to the conviction that a clash of doctrines is an opportunity for Christian faith, we will consider specific examples of Western and non-Western challenges.

THE CHURCH AND
WOMEN'S LIBERATION

Of the many opportunities for creative transformation afforded by the achievements of Western civilization, one of the most challenging is that posed by the new self-consciousness of women. Their movement for liberation is still in process, and the many creative insights it has generated have not yet attained any settled order. But they have already raised to clear consciousness the fact that we live in a male-dominated society, composed of male-dominated institutions, and that this male domination conspicuously characterizes the churches. Practical questions of justice are forcefully raised, and each of the churches must struggle with these in its own way.

But the women's movement has perceived from the first that the problem is not to be settled through the adjustment of social practices alone. These practices reflect the deep internalization of ideas that are oppressive and would continue to be oppressive even if outward changes were made. At a time when many within the churches had supposed theology was of little importance, perceptive women have seen that the overwhelmingly male character of theological ideas, images, and language have played and continue to play a central role in the oppression of women and of the feminine aspect of all people.

The distinction of the two sexes and of the two principles is important. The need is both to liberate women to be themselves and to play their roles in society freely as human beings, and to liberate the feminine principle in both women and men. But the relation between these two goals is complex, and women rightly fear that men, in seizing onto the latter, may co-opt the movement for their own healing without making the further changes required if women as women are to enter fully into society. Only when women attain an equal place with men in a society that honors the feminine principle equally with the masculine one will the needed changes have been achieved. Finally the received distinction of the feminine and masculine principles must itself be transformed, for it has been shaped from the male standpoint and imposed upon women, and it inhibits both sexes from clear vision and just action. With this general understanding in view, process theology can enter the discussion to make its contribution to the required transformations of Christian teaching. It can do so at the three levels mentioned above: ideas, images, and language. Clearly, at this time male representatives of this theology can do no more than make tentative proposals to the ongoing discussion with the women's movement, but it is appropriate for process theology to enter into this process.

Ideas: The topic was broached in Chapter 3 chiefly at the ontological level. At that level process theology is already far advanced. Whitehead's understanding of God was shaped against the view that God acts on the world but receives nothing from it, that he is wholly self-sufficient, and that his agency is that of compulsion. (Here we have used the masculine pronoun advisedly.) Thus Whitehead was rejecting from his metaphysical idea of God elements that are stereotypically masculine. Against them he stresses God's responsive love, God's tenderness, and God's sharing of human suffering, and he grounds these images metaphysically. In the resultant metaphysical idea of God there is a shift in the balance from traditionally masculine attributes to traditionally feminine ones.

Images: Of course no theologian has asserted that God is ontologically male, but the understanding of God in terms of masculine attributes has been associated with almost exclusively male images of God. It is images that shape the personal life and vision of believers, and it is the particular work of theology to clarify and responsibly transmit these images. This responsibility is both to the reality as it is best conceptually clarified and to the effect in the lives of people as this can be discerned and anticipated. In the past, the male images of God were appropriate to the reality as conceptually affirmed. Protests against the existential effects of the traditional images were not uncommon and sometimes led to atheism or anti-Christian religious movements, but the protest was rarely explicitly directed against the maleness of the images. Carl Jung was one of the first to note the psychological impoverishment resulting from the lack of female images of God, and to commend the Roman Catholic Church for its semi-deification of Mary. Today it is clear that Mariology alone does not achieve the needed balance, but Jung's point remains valid.

Given Whitehead's metaphysical doctrine of God, theological responsibility no longer favors male images. Given our present understanding of the damage that is done by exclusively male images, theological responsibility requires the encouragement of female images. But there is no simple move from the need of a certain kind of image to its emergence. Images must express real sensibilities and experience, and only as these change can female images emerge on an equal footing with the male ones. On the other hand, the change of sensibility can be aided by experimentation with proposed images. An intermediate step to the use of explicitly female images is the use of images that lend themselves to emphasis on the feminine without insisting upon it. Whitehead's image of the divine patience and tenderness, the one who suffers with us, the one who saves us in the sense of keeping us everlastingly safe, the final unity that takes all things into itself, lean in the direction of the feminine. The images of the great companion and the final wisdom are at least open to feminine interpretation. Further, all these images have Biblical justification, and other images from the New Testament, such as the Comforter and the indwelling Spirit, can be renewed. Perhaps from the use of this kind of image, more explicitly feminine images of deity will emerge naturally.

The feminine and masculine images of God in dipolar theism tend to cluster around the Consequent and Primordial Natures, respectively, and these can be identified with the Spirit and the Logos. But process theology cannot be satisfied with a simple association of stereotypically feminine traits with the Spirit and masculine ones with the Logos. The Spirit is profoundly active and directive as an agent and ruling principle in the church. And Whitehead formulates his account of the Primordial Nature of God as it works in the world as an explicit rejection of stereotypically masculine attributes. He attacks the church for having retained the deeper idolatry "of the fashioning of God in the image of the Egyptian, Persian, and Roman rulers," thereby giving "unto God the attributes which belonged exclusively to Caesar." (*PR* 520.) When he juxtaposes to this his own image, derived from Jesus, "of the tender elements of the world, which slowly and in quietness operate by love" *(ibid.),* he still has primarily in view the Primordial Nature.

Language: At the level of language the problem is peculiarly urgent and recalcitrant. It is urgent because language shapes images and hence affects our actual sensibility and modes of perception. Exclusively masculine language about God distorts our images and represses women. The problem is recalcitrant because language must develop out of shared usage rather than by the fiat of theologians. At this level process theology can stress that language is in process and that it does change as new understandings and images emerge. Process theology can contribute to the new understanding and support new images. By circumlocutions and other devices, process theologians can avoid the heavy use of male language in their own writing about deity—as we have tried to do in this book. Further, we can participate in the ongoing conversation within the church, encouraging the emergence of forms of language about God which both reflect and support more adequate images.

By working in the areas of ideas, images, and language, process theology can encourage the churches to participate in the church by heeding the call of Christ to be creatively transformed and thereby become the spearhead, rather than a reluctant follower, of the movement to bring full equality to women and the feminine principle. The value of process thought in the area of ideas has already been recognized by feminist theologians. (See Mary Daly, *Beyond God the Father: Toward a Philosophy of Women's Liberation* [Beacon Press, Inc., 1973], p. 188.) It is now time to work in the more difficult realms of images and language.

The Church and Buddhism

The encounter with the many movements of creative transformation that have swept the West largely outside the church is profoundly demanding. But the church faces a still more radical challenge. In the movements within the West the church recognizes its own children even when they most strongly oppose it. The spirit that animates these movements insofar as they are truly creative is the spirit of Christ incognito. The liberation of women is the long-delayed realization of the meaning of the Christian truth that *in Christ* there is neither male nor female. Hence, in transforming itself in its response to such movements, the church reunites itself with its own true self from which, through fear, it has alienated itself.

But today the church faces a more radical task. It has become increasingly aware of the great achievements of ancient traditions that the church once dismissed as pagan. Especially the great religious movements of India and China capture the Western imagination and demand attention. These are emphatically *not* children of the church. They are older than the church and had proven their worth before the church was born. The spirit that breathes through them is other than the spirit of the church, but it is an otherness that commands respect and admiration.

The church faced an analogous task in its early years in its encounter with Greek culture and especially with the great Greek philosophies. Some Christians claimed that these were children of Old Testament Judaism, but for the most part Christians recognized their otherness. As other, some rejected them as evil, but some saw in the other something they wanted to claim for Christ. These won out, and over a period of centuries the otherness of Greek philosophy was critically assimilated into a creatively transformed Christianity.

Despite the great achievements of such thinkers as Augustine and Thomas, the process of creative synthesis is never finished. Classicists rightly confront the synthesis with aspects of the Greek achievement that it distorted and omitted. Biblical scholars similarly confront the synthesis with its failure to do justice to the Old and New Testaments. Further, the critical appropriation was often not sufficiently critical. Process theology is another in the long line of attempts to transform the synthesis so as to be both internally more coherent and more adequate to what now appear as the important insights of each of the synthesized traditions. Process theology assumes that, even if it succeeds in transforming the dominant philosophical-theological tradition, it will not bring the process to a conclusion. On the contrary, it looks forward to its own creative transformation into something else.

While continuing to submit itself to creative transformation in its assimilation of new aspects of Western culture, Christianity needs to open itself to still more radical transformation through the Asian religions. The task is to be carried out individually with each of these great Ways, but the conversation with Buddhism is particularly urgent and fruitful.

Whitehead saw that his philosophy of process had special congeniality with some streams of Oriental thought. With Buddhism it shares in the denial of substance. Buddhism draws conclusions from this denial that are religiously far removed from the Western Christian tradition. Process theology has been shaped in its fundamental spirit by this latter tradition. Does this mean that process theology has failed to follow to the end the implications of its own insights? Must it learn from Buddhism its own deeper religious meaning?

Consider first the understanding of the human person. The usual Western view has been that there is an entitative self, or a subject of experience and action. The word "I" has referred ultimately to this transcendental or underlying self. It is this self whose salvation is sought and who is held accountable for deeds.

Whitehead and Buddhists alike deny the existence of this self. In this they resemble the existentialists, but they go farther. Heidegger, for example, thinks of a single human existence or *Dasein* from birth to death. Thus the person as this *Dasein* has real existence as a unitary entity. Both Whitehead and Buddhism hold that this *Dasein* is only a strand of experiences in the total flux of experiences. The real entities are the individual experiences. The mode of connection that constitutes them as a single person is secondary to their individuality.

Buddhists know that intellectual acquiescence in this theory of the person does not entail existential realization of its truth. People who believe it to be true continue to act as if their personal identity through time were an ontological given. To this failure of realization Buddhism traces human suffering. Hence it has devised meditations through which the power of illusion can be broken and people can know who and what they are. To do this they must stop interpreting their experience and simply let their experience be what it is. What it is is *sunyata,* which is probably best translated as "emptiness." It is the coming together of what is not. To realize this is to be free from anxiety about one's supposed past or future or even present. There is no one about whom to worry.

From an external perspective there is a series of such coming-togethers. But from the internal perspective there is no series. There is only the event. At all times the real perspective is the internal one, for the unconscious supposition that we can stand outside the stream of events and observe them is false. For many purposes it is necessary to speak as if this public world were real, but the ultimate and true standpoint is always within the empty event of coming together. In that perspective there is no past and future and hence no time. There is only happening.

All of this is intelligible for a Whiteheadian, but it had not been perceived or understood in this way apart from the encounter with Buddhism. Process theology has generally assumed that most of the religious and ethical implications of personal existence were preserved in its analysis of personal identity as dominant inheritance from the past and transmission to the future. It has generally supported common sense, calling attention to those features of common sense which oppose a self-identical self underlying experience, and it has corrected fallacious interpretations of common sense. But it has stressed that the empirical identity through time is real and valuable. We saw how it wrestles to preserve the values of the person in its eschatology.

Whereas Buddhist thought takes its stand within what Whitehead calls the process of prehensive unification, or concrescence, Whitehead begins with the analysis of the temporal process from without, in terms of transition. When in *Process and Reality* he turned to the analysis of concrescence, he adopted in part the perspective of concrescence, but his analysis throughout is informed by his prior study of transition. Alone among major philosophers of East or West he finds among the components of concrescence other units of process. Whitehead thereby grounds within concrescence itself its temporal relation to the past, although he agrees with the Buddhist that the unit of process, the actual occasion, is not a temporal process. Apart from its inclusion of other units of process, the concrescence is, as the Buddhist affirms, out of time.

Another difference between Whitehead and the Buddhist analysis is that Whitehead wants to locate within concrescence all the elements needed to explain ordinary experience, whereas the Buddhist seeks in concrescence freedom from many of these elements. For example, Whitehead looks for the elements of purpose and choice in concrescence itself and accordingly identifies subjective aim and decision as universal aspects of concrescence with particularly important roles. Buddhists, if they acknowledge such elements at all, attribute to them no special importance. Whatever is there, is there, signifying nothing and explaining nothing.

The encounter with Buddhism forces the process theologian to see more clearly the extent to which Whitehead's philosophical analysis itself is informed by Christian interests. Clearly, when the analysis of experience is informed by Buddhist interests instead, it yields different results. The two sets of results need not be contradictory. Everything the Buddhist finds may be there to be found, and everything Whitehead finds may be there to be found. For this reason the encounter with Buddhism can lead to a creative transformation of process theology that does not deny its insights but incorporates them in a larger whole. Perhaps it can adopt from Buddhism the art of meditation while transforming it into an instrument of a new form of Christianity.

What the results will be for the appreciation of personal existence can not be foreseen. But some speculations can be based on beginnings already made. Whitehead in his account of Peace envisioned an overcoming of the limitations of personality in a wider coordination of interests. He falsely suspected Buddhism of settling for anaesthesia. The enlightened Buddhist is capable of an inclusive awareness denied to most of us. The Buddhist can be totally present without anxiety. Thus what Buddhists attain by discipline is much like what Christians, including Whitehead, ask as a gift.

Differences remain. It seems that Christian Peace is an expansion of care for self to care for others. In this extension the perception of individual existence through time plays a role in the discrimination of important elements in the environment. The resultant Peace supports judgments of better and worse and discriminating involvement in social causes. Buddhists arrive at their similar results by overcoming care for their own past and future. They learn to cease discriminating the relative value or importance of the ingredients of their immediate experience. This renders them radically open, radically present, radically compassionate without discrimination. In encounter with Buddhism, Christians may be able to shape new visions of the future. The ideal of new Christian communities of mutual participation in Chapter 7, while not Buddhist, reflects the influence of Buddhism.

The question about persons is bound up with the question about God. The Buddhist is indifferent toward those features of our experience which lead Whitehead to speak of God, i.e., purpose, accountability, qualitative novelty, order supportive of the emergence of intensities, and gradations of value. Thus Buddhists are not led by their experience to belief in Whitehead's God. But it would be too strong a statement to say that Buddhism necessarily denies the existence of God as Whitehead conceives deity.

Buddhism often speaks against belief in God, but by God it understands an ultimate ground of being, a substance underlying and relativizing the flux of events, or a static being transcending the flux. Process theology denies God in these senses too. In place of an ultimate ground of being Whitehead speaks of creativity as ultimate. But creativity, far from having eminent supratemporal reality, has no existence in itself and is to be found only in actual instances of the many becoming one. In place of a substance or static being underlying or transcending the flux, Whitehead speaks of God as a formative element of the flux. It is true that he speaks of a primordial, eternal nature of God, but this envisagement of possibilities is an abstraction from the actual process that is God. Since the questions to which God is the answer are not usual Buddhist questions, Whitehead's God is not to be found in Buddhism, but divinities with somewhat analogous cosmological and religious functions do appear in the Buddhist literature. The question of divine realities in a nonsubstantial and processive sense is for Buddhism metaphysically open.

Just because of the possibility of discussing this processive God with Buddhists, process theology must question how fully it has reflected on the meaning of the nonsubstantial character of God. Has it not continued to image God philosophically and religiously in ways that grow out of the traditions of Being and substance? How fully does it religiously realize the meanings of its own affirmations? The encounter with Buddhism will assist us in answering these questions.

One example of the illumination that Buddhism may bring to process theology is through its doctrines of emptiness. The ideal for the Buddhist is the nothingness of perfect emptiness. In Whiteheadian terms the individual actual occasion is to realize itself as a void that interposes nothing to the many that would constitute it as one. Practically, this means that the occasion voids itself of self-definition and delimiting aim so as to allow what-is to fill it. The aim is to achieve an optimal fullness by interposing no principle of selection.

Whitehead's account of the kingdom of heaven or the Consequent Nature of God has remarkable affinities to this Buddhist view. Because the divine aim is at the realization of all possibilities in due season, it interposes no particular principle of selection upon the Consequent Nature. Each element is allowed to be what it is. "Thus the consequent nature of God is composed of a multiplicity of elements with individual self-realization. It is just as much a multiplicity as it is a unity; it is just as much one immediate fact as it is an unresting advance beyond itself." (*PR* 53.) This is possible because the "perfection of God's subjective aim, derived from the completeness of his primordial nature issues into the character of his consequent nature. In it there is no loss, no obstruction." (*PR* 524.) God is "empty" of "self" insofar as "self" is understood as an essence that can be preserved only by excluding "other" things, or at least not allowing them to be received just as they are. How would it affect our religious sensibilities if we thought of the kingdom of heaven as the everlasting divine *sunyata?* Would this not support, by radicalizing, the ideal of responsive love?

These comments are intended to indicate that process theology is in process. The outcome of that process cannot be foretold, and indeed there will not be some finished outcome, only new processes. But process theology may have as its special contribution to the Christian church the ability to open itself freely and perceptively to the other and lead the church in the resulting creative transformation. To this end its capacity to understand Buddhism and be transformed through it may have particular importance.

9

THE GLOBAL CRISIS AND A THEOLOGY OF SURVIVAL

Chapter 8 treated women's liberation as a challenge to Christianity arising in the orbit of its own influence and Buddhism as a challenge that comes radically from without. The growing awareness that human survival is genuinely and even imminently threatened provides a third challenge that transcends the distinction of West and East. The sensitivities of process theology prepare it to make a distinctive contribution to the response to this challenge as well. Indeed, much in the earlier chapters was written with an eye to this overarching challenge. This chapter, therefore, serves to summarize process theology as well as to apply it to the global crisis. If the churches refuse to be transformed in the light of this crisis, they will be denying the most basic call of God, the call to life itself.

Of the many themes involved in a theology of survival, four will be discussed here: (1) the spatiotemporal scale; (2) the human and the natural; (3) ecological sensitivity; and (4) responsibility and hope. On each point process theology discerns truth in the major competing positions or attitudes, but it finds that in their characteristic expressions they lead to death rather than to life. The task is to frame a creative synthesis that includes the complex truth in a larger whole that makes for life.

THE SPATIOTEMPORAL SCALE

The time scale of the Bible and of most Christians through the Reformation period was highly compressed. It was commonly supposed that the creation of the universe took place only a few thousand years before Christ and that the end of the world was imminent. Similarly the space scale was small. This planet was viewed as the center of the universe with all else revolving about it.

The space-time scale of the imagination in India, by contrast, is infinitely enlarged. There is no beginning and no end, or, if this cosmic epoch had a beginning unimaginably long ago and moves toward an end in an equally distant future, this epoch is but one of infinitely many. Similarly, our world is but one of an infinite number of worlds.

The deep religious meanings of these opposed scales continues to express itself in the cultures of East and West. The West has a sense of urgency, of the importance of historical events, of movement toward an end that somehow justifies what is done in the present. The East relativizes the importance of present occurrences and expects from the future nothing that will make sense of the suffering of the present. Serenity is achieved in a psychic withdrawal that then makes possible action in the world without attachment to its results.

Neither attitude is adequate in face of our global crisis. The foreshortened time scale of the West leads to crash programs to solve immediate problems such as world hunger without consideration of the wide-ranging, long-term consequences of these efforts. Economic development is encouraged in terms of five-year plans that ignore the foreseeable consequences even on the scale of fifty years. Economic theory systematically discounts the more distant future, thus justifying the continuing rape of resources for short-term profit.

But the patience of the Eastern spirit and its resignation in the face of outward calamity are of no greater help. There is real urgency about the problem of survival that is not adequately responded to by the cultivation of a serene mind and detached action. Reliance on habitual patterns is often not as destructive as inappropriate technological innovations, but it too leads to misery and destruction. In fact, the Eastern lands are in general ruled by a largely Westernized elite; on this basis they maintain their independence and play their role in world affairs.

Scientific cosmology challenges both the Western and the Eastern imagination. Against the Biblical view, it expands the history of our cosmos to billions of years and shows our planet as but a tiny speck circling a middle-sized star in one of many galaxies. But both Christians and post-Christian humanists have resisted allowing this scientific picture significantly to alter their sensibilities. Even if our planet has existed for billions of years and the human species for millions, history is dated from the rise of civilization, and that corresponds roughly to the Biblical chronology of creation. History is contrasted with nature, which is portrayed as essentially changeless and unimportant except as the stage and resource for history. Indeed, philosophical idealism even assures us that, since human experience is the only true reality, the scientific picture of its late emergence on the scene is ultimately to be reversed. The scientific picture is to be viewed as a part of history and not as pointing to its relativization. Characteristically this allows for concentration on short-term historical goals with little concern that the end of history may in no sense be an End.

Whereas in the West the scientific picture is a threat to the centrality of the human drama and the importance of historical acts, in the East it is a threat to the sense of infinities. It challenges the Eastern imagination by indicating that the human species appeared at most only a few million years ago and that conditions of settled life arose much more recently. Against the view that there are infinities of other planets on which similar events occur, science suggests that the conditions that made advanced forms of life possible on this planet are very special ones indeed. The extreme minimization of the importance of the course of history is qualified. The nuclear poisoning of the planet or the destruction of its ozone shield against the harmful rays of the sun has the kind of decisive significance that the traditional Indian imagery was intended to rule out.

Process theology intends to think through the meaning for our existence and actions of the space-time scales that scientific cosmology suggests. It affirms that there was real value and enjoyment in the eons of time before high forms of life appeared anywhere in the universe, but that the level and importance of enjoyment increased greatly when, on this planet (and wherever else a similar development may have occurred) animals and finally humans emerged. It recognizes in the multiplication of the numbers of humans an increase in the potential of high forms of enjoyment that are intrinsically valuable. It sees that species have risen and perished before and that a similar fate may befall the human species, but it does not regard this with detached indifference. On the contrary, this would mean the loss of something of peculiar value that is probably unique in the entire universe. Furthermore, there is danger that, unlike any other species, human beings may involve all high forms of life on this planet in their destruction. Thus the products of billions of years of evolutionary development are threatened in a future that is to be understood in terms of decades. There is no reason to expect that this impoverished planet could again develop to its present biotic richness or that the values achieved in some other place or time could render negligible the loss caused by the premature death of high forms of life on our planet. The sense of urgency is justified, but it must not be translated into crash programs to solve local and temporary needs. It must find form in a breakthrough into a completely new way of living that can make possible a decent survival for the human species in a rich and supportive biological context.

THE HUMAN AND THE NATURAL

The Western contrast of history and nature has some roots in the Bible, especially in the minor concern for nature in the New Testament. However, in the extreme form noted in the preceding section, it is a modern product. Just at the point in history when human activity was beginning to raise global threats to the human environment, the Western imagination was distracted from attention to nature by the theoretical reduction of nature to a function of human experience or a static, intrinsically valueless condition for dynamic human action. Even now, when the dangers are too manifest to be entirely overlooked, Westerners propose that they should be solved by programs of exploitation of resources that hardly differ from the ones that have led to the trouble.

Among the most sensitive Christians there is quick, positive reaction to the call for human justice and liberation. But there is deep resistance to noticing that justice and freedom are of little value to the starving and that in many parts of the world the land will not support a continuing rapid increase of population. Against these points, the most concerned Christians are likely to rationalize their conviction that the solution is to be found in the realm of history, and that nature can be counted on to supply the necessary resources. Any proposal to limit population growth by government regulations so as to make ossible a viable future is quickly criticized for its threats to personal liberty, if not on the moralistic grounds that any interference with reproductive processes is "sin." Any concern for the welfare of animal species other than the human is quickly written off as sentimental and as insensitive to the pressing needs of human beings. At most what is accepted is an idea of stewardship that in fact reduces all that is not human to a means to human ends.

In sharp reaction against the radically anthropocentric stance of humanists and most Christians, others are calling for the full recognition of the human species as simply one among many with no more rights than any of the others. They speak of a "democracy of value." The idealized image that is affirmed in these circles is that of a harmony and balance among the species that was disrupted by the rise of agriculture and especially by civilization. The hunting and gathering society represented the stage of human development in which natural forces determined the balance among the several species and the biosphere as a whole could flourish. It was also the condition in which human beings were in fullest harmony with their own bodily needs and rhythms. The

course of history, in this view, has been one long denial of human
bodily reality and a progressive destruction of the biosphere.
Process theology sees truth both in the focus on history as the
important arena and in the radical condemnation of this focus.
Human history *is* the locus of the most important events on this
planet. It is to secure its continuation, above all, that radical change
is needed. But history has been built too much on the denial of
bodily reality, and it has involved a progressive destruction of the
biosphere that makes it possible. Human beings do have unique
value and worth that is probably not equalled by any other species
on this planet. But other species also have intrinsic worth, and in
some instances great worth. Their survival and free development
is important also, not only when it contributes to that of human
beings but even when it involves some cost to the human species.

It is often supposed that once the dualism of the human and the
natural is abandoned, as by process theology, no rational grounds
remain for the discussion of values and rights on an inter-species
basis. It is charged that any discussion of value in the nonhuman
world can only be an expression of human liking or of similarity
to the human. This is not true for process theology. Value is found
in enjoyment, and enjoyment is a characteristic of all living beings.
But the capacity for enjoyment varies. A world reduced to radioac-
tive rock, sand, and water would be extremely impoverished, even
if a few unicellular organisms survived. It would be richer if insect
life survived, and richer still if there were reptiles and birds. We
do not even know, of course, precisely how much capacity for
enjoyment is possessed by other human beings. Clearly, our ability
to conjecture the relative capacity for enjoyment of dolphins and
orangutans is still less. But we are not devoid of reasonable guesses
in this area, and it is possible to gather information that enables us
to refine these guesses into intelligent judgments.

Process theology gives ontological grounding for the now widespread recognition of the importance of the human body. It shows
how enjoyment arises out of the body as its condition, and how
indeed much of our enjoyment is the enjoyment of the body's
enjoyment. The Christian suppression of the body long associated
with the dualism of history and nature gave rise to distinctive and

valuable forms of spirituality that should not be deplored or entirely abandoned. But the pressing need today is to adapt these achievements to the renewed appreciation of our bodiliness. To recover a harmonious relation to the rhythms of the body is an avenue to harmony with the rhythms of nature in general. Such harmony can undergird, renew, and transform the high forms of spirituality that were first achieved through the repression of bodily enjoyment.

The overcoming of the dualism of history and nature can open us to the recognition that nature has a history. Far from being endlessly repetitive and cyclical, as the dualists have liked to think, life on this planet, and even the cosmos as a whole, has been in constant nonrepetitive movement. Continents have drifted, weather has changed, and species have evolved. Further, the changes of nature and of history have been intimately interconnected. Changes in weather have led to movements of peoples, and actions of people have changed the condition of the land. Empires have fallen as they have destroyed their own agricultural base. Learning to read the story of the human past in terms of the decisive role of nature will help us to break our dualistic habits and to interpret our present actions in the light of their natural-historical meaning and consequences.

What process theology now seeks is a form of human-historical progress that simultaneously allows for the meeting of real human needs and for the renewed development of a rich and complex biosphere. It therefore opposes, first, that form of "progress" which continues to destroy wholesale other living things and thereby their enjoyment and the context for future human enjoyment. It opposes also the ideal of returning to an earlier stage of human development. This would necessitate unparalleled suffering and inhumanity leading to the drastically reduced number of people that could be supported in the more primitive state. Process theology holds that science guided by imaginative vision can find ways whereby a relatively large (though certainly limited) human population can enter into new and finer forms of enjoyment that are compatible with sharing the earth with many other species. There is hope in the visions of some ecologically sensitive agriculturists and in the architectural ecologies (arcologies) of Paolo Soleri. But such hopes can be realized only if there are fundamental changes away from what is now valued and from the life-styles and forms of social organization to which we are accustomed. Frugality and communality must replace conspicuous consumption and individualism. Jesus' glorification of poverty has new relevance, and indeed there is much in our Christian tradition lately ignored that can be brought into the service of new ideals. We have pointed out previously, especially in Chapters 1 and 4, ways in which process theology supports a transvaluation of values in the direction that is needed.

Process theology in this way combines the norms of evolutionists and ecologists. Evolutionists characteristically see value chiefly in the growing edge of the process, and therefore in the human species. If the further course of human evolution requires the decimation of other species, this is a sacrifice they accept. Ecologists, on the other hand, see the mutual dependence of species in such light that the advance of a single species at the expense of others appears destructive of the larger whole. They relish the rich complexity of mutually supportive species and suspect that each has a distinctive and ultimately irreplaceable role to play in the whole. They are fearful of further human "progress."

Process theology holds that ecologists are right in their concern to stop the decimation of species and the simplification of the biosphere. Ecologists often argue for this on a too-limited basis; for it is not the case that all existing species are needed for the sake of the others. Especially the larger animal species can in some cases be destroyed without significant danger to the biosphere. But this destruction is still rightly sensed as a loss. Further, the loss cannot be adequately understood simply as a denial of the opportunity for human beings or other observers to experience that species.

The intuition that the destruction of species and the simplification of the biosphere entails loss implicitly witnesses to the sense that the universe is an inclusive unity. It implies that this inclusive unity is a locus of value; that means that it is an integrated subject. Whitehead speaks of our prereflective sense of the value of all things for the whole in these terms:

There is a unity in the universe, enjoying value and (by its immanence) sharing value. For example, take the subtle beauty of a flower in some isolated glade of a primeval forest. No animal has ever had the subtlety of experience to enjoy its full beauty. And yet this beauty is a grand fact in the universe. When we survey nature and think however flitting and superficial has been the animal enjoyment of its wonders, and when we realize how incapable the separate cells and pulsations of each flower are of enjoying the total effect—then our sense of the value of the details for the totality dawns upon our consciousness. This is the intuition of holiness, the intuition of the sacred, which is at the foundation of all religion. (*MT* 119–120.)

This prereflective awareness of the unity of the world becomes an explicit awareness in process thought. God is the unified experience of all things. God is impoverished when the rich complexity of the biosphere is reduced.

Evolutionists are correct that the human species can probably contribute the greatest enjoyment of all, but they are wrong if they deduce from this that the sacrifice of other species for the human advance is unimportant. Human enjoyment may be greater than enjoyment on the part of elephants and hence make a greater contribution to God. But the greatest enjoyment requires contrasts and contrasts of contrasts. The divine experience is most enriched as it receives the widest variety of types of enjoyment. To simplify, even for the sake of the individually most important contributor, is still to impoverish. This appeal to God simply brings to consciousness our prereflective sense that we live not only for our own enjoyment but also for the Whole of which we are parts.

ECOLOGICAL SENSITIVITY

Traditional Christian understanding has been bound up with a unilinear view of the explanation of events. This view has been manifest especially in the understanding of the human person. It has lifted up the single succession of experiences from birth to death and heightened self-consciousness of their personal unity within this succession. Individual self-identity through time has become so self-evident that it is assumed to be metaphysically given. Any events not a part of this succession, including all the events in the body, are conceived as having only external relations to this unilinear sequence.

Unilinear thinking also characterizes the traditional understanding of Biblical history. Of course one knew that there were other historical events as well, but "sacred history"—the only meaning-giving history—moves from creation to eschaton through a single strand of events. Concurrent events are only background to these. It is these and these alone that decisively periodize history.

Unilinear thinking long characterized science as well. Scientists have sought "the cause" of the occurrence that interested them. The cause was sharply distinguished from the conditions that were taken to be given and of little interest. Similarly courts of law and ethicists have attempted to fix responsibility on someone's act as "the cause" of a harmful state of affairs.

Unilinear thinking prevails in planning and in technology. A goal or end-in-view is established, the steps needed to reach the goal are determined, the necessary means are obtained, and the process is initiated. Other consequences of these steps than the one in view are treated as incidental.

In modern scientific and historical work this unilinear thinking has gradually eroded. It is increasingly recognized that each event arises from the intersection of numerous more-or-less canalized processes. There is no isolable cause of any occurrence. Recognizing this, the tendency has been to give up the search for causes altogether. One can only describe what occurs. In science, this usually takes the form of mathematical formulae; in history, of individual accounts. But the difference is one of degree.

The replacement of causal explanation with description marks an advance, in that it recognizes the distortion involved in unilinear accounts. It leads to a deep change of spirit in which what-is can be accepted as it is without the restless quest to understand, control, and change. This shift has cut deeply into a major segment of the Western elite and expresses itself in many forms. Alan Watts gives powerful expression to it in his account of a psychedelic revelation:

The sense of the world becomes totally obvious. I am struck with amazement that I or anyone could have thought life a problem or being a mystery. I call to everyone to gather round.

Listen, there's something I *must* tell. I've never, never seen it so clearly. But it doesn't matter a bit if you don't understand, because each one of you is quite perfect as you are, even if you don't know it. Life is basically a gesture, but no one, no thing, is *making* it. There is no necessity for it to happen, and none for it to go on happening. For it isn't being driven by anything; it just happens freely of itself. It's a gesture of motion, of sound, of color, and just as no one is making it, it isn't *happening* to anyone. There is simply no problem of life; it is completely purposeless play—exuberance which is its own end. Basically there is the gesture. Time, space, and multiplicity are complications of it. There is no reason whatever to explain it, for explanations are just another form of complexity, a new manifestation of life on top of life, of gestures gesturing. Pain and suffering are simply extreme forms of play, and there isn't anything in the whole universe to be afraid of because it doesn't happen to anyone! (*The Joyous Cosmology* [Vintage Books, 1965], pp. 70 ff.)

Process theology can understand this vision but it cannot accept its message as the final word. Things are not simply as they are if this means: what they had to be. They are what they have chosen to be in the context of possibility established by their environments. We are part of one another's environments, and the way we constitute ourselves and act through our bodies influences the possibilities others will have for enjoyment. As James Douglass notes, Watts' message comes from a California country estate. It does not ring true in a *favela* in São Paulo, where misery is real. (James W. Douglass, *Resistance and Contemplation* [Doubleday & Company, Inc., 1972], p. 131.)

This is to say that process theology cannot share in the abandonment of ethical and legal questions which is entailed by the rejection of causal thinking. Each of us must understand that how we use our freedom affects the opportunities of others as well as our own future. But process theology does share in the rejection of unilinear causal thinking. It calls for an ecological sensibility.

Ecology teaches us that causal relations are real but far from unilinear. Each event in an ecological system is made possible by a complex interconnection of antecedent events. No one of the antecedents is "the cause" of the event, but all of them play a causal role. Whitehead shows that these ecological relationships are not peculiar to certain biological phenomena but are universal throughout the actual world. Every occurrence grows out of its whole environment and becomes a part of the environment out of which all future events come into being. In the constitution of one event, certain others play a particularly large role; so discrimination of relative importance is possible. But the full causal explanation of any occurrence is infinitely complex, as are its full causal consequences.

Causal efficacy is a mode of immanence and of participation. Insofar as we influence one another, we participate in one another, and through all sorts of complex patterns all of us influence one another. This is a part of our prereflective knowledge that comes to expression from time to time in spite of our normal conscious adherence to a conceptuality that denies it. John Donne reminds us that "no man is an island" and that every man's death diminishes each of us. Process theology hopes that, when we lift up this element in our prethematized consciousness to full conceptual clarity and affirmation, our awareness of participation in one another will be heightened so that it will again shape our deepest sensitivities and responses to one another. If so, it will be the recovery at a new level of what was present in primitive tribal experience. The new level will recognize that the "tribe" is now the whole of humanity. The starvation of an Indian peasant will be felt to diminish each one of us.

This mode of relatedness differs from the ethical one but need not replace it. The ethical person recognizes that the other has a right to exist and to have enjoyment and that this right lays a claim upon her or him. One is obligated so to order one's life as to facilitate the enjoyment of others. One seeks to conform one's life to the disinterested concern for others. The sense of mutual participation reduces the sense of the difference between self and other. Just as one's concerns for the well-being of one's own body is at once for the sake of the body and for the sake of the experiencing human subject, so also one's concern for the well-being of one in whose existence one participates is both for the sake of the other and for one's own sake. As the sensitivity increases, the ethical imperative becomes less important. But because the sense of participation wavers and tends to be selective, it needs to be guided, encouraged, and supplemented by the ethical norm.

Process theology calls for still further extension of the sense of participation. The whole of nature participates in us and we in it. We are diminished not only by the misery of the Indian peasant but also by the slaughter of whales and porpoises, and even by the "harvesting" of the giant redwoods. We are diminished still more when the imposition of temperate-zone technology onto tropical agriculture turns grasslands into deserts that will support neither human nor animal life.

Insofar as we are transformed in our self-understanding from unilinear beings with only external relations to the rest of the world into participants in the whole process of nature-history, planning and the use of technology will be transformed. We will no longer habitually focus upon a single end-in-view and judge all means in terms of that end. Rather we will consider every action in terms of the whole scope of its probable and even possible consequences. We will take account of the whole context out of which our action must grow. We will refrain from those actions which might have irreversible negative consequences upon the life-support system of the planet even at considerable personal sacrifice and even when the likelihood is slight or unknown. Hence we will abandon most of our present technological solutions and release our imaginations to find instead comprehensive approaches to changed ways of life and changed ways of obtaining necessary goods.

Whitehead's reformulation of the notion of perfection is "the notion of that power in history which implants into the form of process, belonging to each historic epoch, the character of a drive towards some ideal, to be realized within that period." (*MT* 120.) The realization of the ideal for our period will mean our creative transformation into beings who can survive, and indeed flourish more abundantly, upon a planet with finite physical resources and other valuable species of life.

RESPONSIBILITY AND HOPE

The changes required for a decent and hopefully enriched survival are enormous. The momentum of our present destructive patterns of production and consumption is overwhelming. If we care deeply about the future of the planet, we are tempted to despair. If those despair who care the most and understand the best, then indeed, there is little hope; for if we despair, we will not participate responsibly in what needs to be done.

All Christian teaching opposes despair, and most Christian teaching intends to encourage responsible participation in what needs to be done. However, it often fails to fulfill its intentions, so that critics of Christianity have rightly accused it of discouraging responsible action. It does this in two main ways.

First, Christian teaching can discourage responsible action by offering confidence in place of hope. If we are to act with the necessary urgency, we need to believe that there are possibilities open in the future that will carry us through our present crisis. But if we are told instead that there is in fact no real danger, that all is in the hands of a good and omnipotent God who will care for us, then the urgency disappears. Confident Christians look with complacent serenity at the activists and chide them for their anxiety. Christ, they assert, overcomes anxiety with the assurance that all will be well. We should each do our bit, but we should avoid the idea that we have individually or collectively any significant responsibility for the outcome. We should live comfortably and confidently, not unduly upsetting people, and certainly avoiding heroics. The implication is that we can continue basically on the course on which we find ourselves, performing our minor duties, and leave the large issues to God.

Second, much modern Christian teaching discourages responsible action by placing the *full* responsibility upon human beings. We are told that God turned the world over to us. This kind of teaching thinks deistically of a God who established the world and the principles by which we should act and then placed us as free agents in that world. In this case the full burden falls upon us and there is no help from God. On this basis we have no reason to expect a future of human action that is radically different from the past, and hence we cannot realistically ground hope. Where there is no hope, there may still be responsibility. But responsibility exercised without hope is a burden too great to bear. It cannot motivate the change of attitude and practice that is needed.

In the Christian community a more complex prereflective understanding of our situation has repeatedly come to expression to moderate these simplistic views. There is both divine grace and human responsibility. Christian action entails both. There is no divine action apart from creaturely action, but equally the divine action is the principle of hope in the creaturely action. Hence we cannot divide up responsibility for an action, supposing that the more God is responsible for what occurs, the less human beings are responsible, or the more human beings are responsible, the less God has to do with it. On the contrary, it is precisely in the freest and most responsible of human actions that the action of God is most clearly discerned.

Whitehead brings the conceptual explanation of these Christian intuitions to clear expression, and he thereby enables process theology to ground the call to responsible action. For process theology the future is truly open, and that means that there is no assurance that human beings will avoid all those means now becoming available to them to destroy themselves. The danger is real, and an attitude of confidence that God will prevent the worst horrors is irresponsible. The God who "permitted" Auschwitz will permit anything the creatures choose to do. God is not another agent alongside the creatures. God acts only in them and through them.

But the fact that the future is truly open also means that self-destruction is not inevitable. God does act in and through the creatures. The openness of the future does not mean simply that it is now unpredictable because of the complexity of the factors or because an element of chance enters it. The future is much more radically open. That which has never been may yet be. What has been until now does not exhaust the realm of possibilities, and because of God some of these yet unrealized possibilities act as effective lures for their embodiment. God offers to us opportunities to break out of our ruts, to see all things differently, to imagine what has never yet been dreamed. God works to open others to respond to the new visions and to implement them. Insofar as we allow God to do so, God makes all things new. Thus God is the ground of our hope.

This means that we should trust God. Trusting God is not assurance that whatever we do, all will work out well. It is instead confidence that God's call is wise and good. It is sensitizing ourselves to this call so that we can be led and guided by it. It is the renewed willingness to give up the security we experience in accustomed ideas and customs and to enter into the adventure of the trusting life, even when we cannot foresee a favorable outcome. Trust is thus true responsibility, the ability to respond to the concrete situation and God's quite specific call within it.

God offers possibilities that would lead us into the new life we need. God lures, urges, and persuades. We decide. If we decide to enter into the reality into which God calls us, we choose life. If we decide to refuse it, we choose death, a continual dying throughout life and a contribution to the planetary death. This context provides urgency to the words attributed to God in Deut. 30:19: "I have set before you life and death, blessing and curse; therefore choose life, that you and your descendants may live." The choice of life, which is the choice of God's call, is the highest freedom in itself and provides the basis for the expansion of freedom. The refusal of life expresses bondage to the past and to the self and it progressively reduces our capacity for freedom and life. Hope grows with the ability to respond; despair grows with the self-chosen closing in of horizons.

To be responsible in this context is not finally to shoulder an unendurable burden. It is to share in the divine adventure in the world. Although its outcome is never assured, and although it entails the sacrifice of many past forms of enjoyment, in itself it is joyful. The one who experiences the joy of this participation in the divine life hopes urgently for success, but accepts the risk that the only reward may be in the joy itself.

Appendix A

❧◈❧

PHILOSOPHY
AND THEOLOGY

Process theology is a philosophical theology. Especially among Protestants, there has always been suspicion of the use of philosophy for the explanation and defense of faith. The argument against this use is a double one. First, there is the substantive point that the use of philosophical systems in theology has in fact obscured and distorted the Biblical faith. With this criticism process theologians agree. Much of our criticism of classical theism is parallel to the objections of those who oppose all forms of philosophical theology. We believe that the use of philosophy by theologians has introduced many distortions into Christian teaching. But we do not believe that such distortion is inevitable. The problem is to find the "right" philosophy.

Second, against our view that the substantive problems have been caused only by particular limitations of individual philosophies, theologians have argued that the use of a philosophy as a natural theology implies that the philosophy has a higher authority than Christian revelation. They assert that while the philosophical theologians verbally correlate faith with revelation, they in effect treat the philosophy as the highest product of revelation. In the language of general and special revelation: if one is using a philosophy—which is the product of general revelation—as the criterion for judging the historic faith, one is refusing the authority of special revelation. In response to this objection, process theology rejects the sharp contrast of general and special revelation. There is a difference of focus as between philosophy and theology, but each is influenced both by God's revelation in nature and in human experience as a whole and by God's revelation in the decisive insights that arose through extraordinary historical occurrences. Process philosophy, for example, is profoundly influenced by Jesus and his reception in the community of faith. Whitehead saw the theological task to be the elucidation of the truths that are implicit in those events so as to illuminate the whole of experience. (*RM* 31.)

The question of the appropriateness of the use of a particular philosophy in the elucidation of Christian faith was a major point of controversy between Karl Barth and Rudolf Bultmann. Barth objected to the use of any philosophy along the lines indicated above. Bultmann insisted that theology needs a well worked out conceptuality to articulate the preconceptual "understanding of existence" that is implicit in Christian faith. If the theologian is to achieve any measure of clarity and consistency, the question is not *whether* to be guided by philosophy, but only *which* philosophy to use. Bultmann's choice of Heidegger's earlier philosophy expounded in *Being and Time* reflects his view as to the nature of the prereflective content of faith. Since he saw this content as including nothing, even implicitly, about God and the world in themselves, he was satisfied with Heidegger's brilliant analysis of the structure of human existence as such. In fact, Bultmann believes that the theological attempt to describe God and/or the world in themselves is an actual distortion of Christian faith. His well-known call for demythologizing Christian theology is best understood as the call to deobjectify it, i.e., to rid it of "objectifying" talk about God and the world.

Bultmann stands in the Kantian tradition with its idealistic interpretation of the world. The only world about which the Kantian can talk is a product of the structures of the human mind, in its theoretical or objectifying function. Kantians hold that the theoretical work of the natural scientist does not tell us anything that corresponds to the structures of the world in itself, i.e., independently of human perception and thought. They think that the advance of science merely tells us more and more about the forms and categories in terms of which we necessarily perceive and think. On the basis of this view, Bultmann sees no need to reconcile the principles of science, e.g., the principle that every event is caused, with the principles of religion and ethics, e.g., that some events are free, i.e., not totally determined by antecedents. It is sufficient that these two principles do not contradict each other, since they are affirmed from different points of view, and are about events in different realms. The statement that some events are free is made from the point of view of the human being as an agent, with ethical concerns, and is an assertion about events in the realm of reality. The statement that all events are caused is made from the point of view of the theoretical observer, and is about the realm of appearance.

Bultmann holds that prethematized Christian faith contains no implications about God and the world in themselves. It is not clear whether this theological position is due to his standing in the Kantian tradition, or whether a philosophy within the Kantian tradition (i.e., Heidegger's) appealed to him because he already held this view of faith. In either case, his understanding of faith and his choice of a philosophy are correlative.

Whitehead's philosophy is both cosmological and theistic. It provides categories for speaking about God and the nonhuman world as they exist independently of human perception and thought. Since we believe that the prereflective content of faith refers to God and the world as well as to human existence, we prize Whitehead's philosophy for its ability to render explicit this prethematized vision of reality.

The need for a cosmological philosophy is confirmed by the incurable realism of human beings. We cannot finally live except *as if* the world exists independently of human experience. Our incurable realism shows that we are directly aware of being in a world of other things which are actual independently of our awareness of them. They are *given* to us, and given as having existence, structure, and qualities apart from our perception of, and thought about, them. This implies that the natural sciences tell us something about reality and not merely about human experience. Accordingly, people cannot be satisfied with theologies that relegate the revelations of science to the status of information about mere appearance, and thereby fail to discuss science in terms of the same set of concepts used to discuss religion, ethics, and aesthetics.

Appendix B

∽✹∾

A GUIDE TO
THE LITERATURE

Process thought has a sufficiently extended history and includes adherents with sufficiently diverse philosophical and theological interests that an accurate introduction would have to involve itself in numerous controversies. The authors of this book have avoided this problem by concentrating on the thought of Alfred North Whitehead himself on the one hand and frankly presenting their own views on the other. This appendix supplements this unified presentation of process theology by indicating the range of writings first of Whitehead himself and then of those who have been influenced by him and have written about him. It includes a brief discussion of the Chicago school, which proved particularly receptive to his influence. Since for many process theologians a major attraction of Whitehead is that he shows how Christian thought can cohere with a comprehensive understanding of reality, the literature described includes general philosophical, scientific, and interdisciplinary writings. Selective emphasis is governed by theological interests. There is no effort to be exhaustive, and for practical reasons our attention is largely limited to books. The more exhaustive bibliographies that are available are listed.

I. ALFRED NORTH WHITEHEAD

Alfred North Whitehead was born in 1861. His father was a vicar of the Church of England, and the son retained an interest in religion throughout his life. Nevertheless, his field of study and teaching through most of his professional career was mathematics.

Mathematics and physics are closely intertwined, and from the side of a mathematician interested in the way mathematics is related to the actual world, Whitehead developed a philosophy of nature. The major treatises of this period are *An Enquiry Concerning the Principles of Natural Knowledge* (Cambridge University Press, 1919) and *The Concept of Nature* (Cambridge University Press, 1920). From the perspective established in these books he found himself dissatisfied with Einstein's formulation of the theory of relativity, which appeared to give space-time precedence over events. He wrote *The Principle of Relativity with Applications to Physical Science* (Cambridge University Press, 1922) to show that a different mathematical formulation could predict the same empirical results as Einstein's special theory of relativity while expressing a more satisfactory view of nature.

Whitehead's broader humanistic interests expressed themselves in occasional essays written throughout his career. The most influential of the earlier essays are collected in *The Aims of Education and Other Essays* (The Macmillan Company, 1929). But sustained treatment of humanistic topics awaited his early retirement from the University of London and his acceptance of a professorship in philosophy at Harvard University. He had previously understood that his philosophy of nature dealt with the world as known without including the knower as an element in what was known. He now shifted to a metaphysical cosmology that included the human knower within the natural world. This made the history of the human knower important to the understanding of the inclusive nature. *Science and the Modern World* (The Macmillan Company, 1925) surveyed Western thought about nature and introduced Whitehead's own cosmological reflections. In this book for the first time he wrote of God, limiting himself, however, to a strictly metaphysical treatment. He asserted that what more is to be known of God is to be learned from the religious experience of the race. Accordingly he wrote *Religion in the Making* (The Macmillan Company, 1926) to explore this experience and the evidence it provides with respect to the nature of God and God's role in the world. We have quoted extensively from this book.

Whitehead was invited to give the Gifford Lectures, which are devoted to natural theology, in 1927–1928. He used this occasion to write what was published in revised form as *Process and Reality* (The Macmillan Company, 1929). This is without question his *magnum opus,* one of the most complex and original philosophical writings of all time. It expresses his mathematical and scientific interests combined with religious, aesthetic, and metaphysical ones in a unified cosmology. The terminology of this book has become standard for the more technical work in process theology.

Four other books provide less difficult openings into Whitehead's thought of this period. *The Function of Reason* (Princeton University Press, 1929) is the least difficult. It deals with reason as the self-discipline of "mentality," the appetite to enjoy possible forms of experience, which is the source of biological and cultural evolution. *Symbolism: Its Meaning and Effect* (The Macmillan Company, 1927) deals primarily with epistemology. The primary form of symbolism is the "symbolic reference" between the two pure modes of perception, causal efficacy and presentational immediacy. Next in importance to *Process and Reality* is *Adventures of Ideas* (The Macmillan Company, 1933). In the four parts of this book, Whitehead traces the way in which ideas of high generality gradually shape society; explains his basic cosmological, metaphysical, and epistemological ideas; and concludes with the basic features of civilized experience. This last part, which treats Truth, Beauty, Art, Adventure, and Peace, is the most important of Whitehead's writings for understanding his views on the ultimate ideals and values of human life. Whitehead's last book, *Modes of Thought* (The Macmillan Company, 1938), presents an overview of his central ideas devoid of most of his technical terms.

Further insights into Whitehead's thought and Whitehead the man can be gained from Lucien Price's *Dialogues of Alfred North Whitehead* (Little, Brown & Company, 1954; The New American Library of World Literature, Inc., 1956). A complete bibliography of Whitehead's writings can be found in Paul A. Schilpp (ed.), *The Philosophy of Alfred North Whitehead* (Tudor Publishing Company, 2d ed., 1951). A bibliography of secondary literature was published in *Process Studies*, Vol. 1, No. 4 (Winter 1971). An updated, corrected, and annotated version will appear in the series *Bibliographies of Famous Philosophers*, edited by Richard H. Lineback and published by the Philosophy Documentation Center.

II. WHITEHEAD'S STUDENTS

Whitehead had a deep influence on his students at Harvard. He did not seek, however, to impose his own developing system of thought upon them, or to encourage them to become disciples. Instead, his influence led them to develop their own ways of thought. As a group, however, they stand out from the general background of American philosophical thought in the 1930's, 1940's, and 1950's by their rejection of the dominant positivistic and analytic modes. Among the more original and influential of Whitehead's students have been Paul Weiss, F. S. C. Northrop, and Susanne K. Langer.

Paul Weiss devoted a distinguished career at Yale to the creation of his own original metaphysics. This metaphysics has important similarities to that of Whitehead but is not intended as a development of Whitehead's thought or formulated as a critique of it. Weiss did more than any other philosopher in the United States to keep metaphysics alive as a discipline during a period when it was out of favor with both the philosophical and the theological communities. Among his many important books are *Reality* (Princeton University Press, 1938); *Nature and Man* (Henry Holt & Company, Inc., 1947); *Modes of Being* (Southern Illinois University Press, 1958); *Religion and Art* (Marquette University Press, 1963); and *The God We Seek* (Southern Illinois University Press, 1964).

F. S. C. Northrop has been professor of the philosophy of law, also at Yale. He has explored humanistic questions widely and deeply, extending Whitehead's incipient interest in the relation of Eastern and Western thought. On this topic he wrote the widely read book *The Meeting of East and West* (The Macmillan Company, 1946). His many other writings include *Science and First Principles* (The Macmillan Company, 1931); *The Logic of the Sciences and the Humanities* (The Macmillan Company, 1947); and *The Complexity of Legal and Ethical Experience: Studies in the Method of Normative Subjects* (Little, Brown & Company, Inc., 1959). Also, in collaboration with Mason W. Gross, he edited *Alfred North Whitehead: An Anthology* (The Macmillan Company, 1961).

Susanne K. Langer has made her greatest contribution in the philosophical reflection on art. She has written *The Practice of Philosophy* (Henry Holt & Company, Inc., 1930) and *Philosophy in a New Key: A Study in the Symbolism of Reason, Rite, and Art* (Harvard University Press, 1942). The latter is dedicated "To Alfred North Whitehead, my great Teacher and Friend." She has also written *Feeling and Form: A Theory of Art* (Charles Scribner's Sons, 1953); *Problems of Art* (Charles Scribner's Sons, 1957); *Philosophical Sketches* (Johns Hopkins Press, 1962); and *Mind: An Essay on Human Feeling* (Johns Hopkins Press, Vol. I, 1967; Vol. II, 1972).

Some other students of Whitehead's Harvard years may be mentioned to indicate the wide range of interests. Charles H. Malik of Lebanon, who, at Harvard University in 1937, wrote his doctoral dissertation under Whitehead on "The Metaphysics of Time in the Philosophies of A. N. Whitehead and M. Heidegger," testifies to his deep indebtedness. Malik later became president of the 13th General Assembly of the United Nations. Winston King has devoted a distinguished career to the study of the history of religions. His books include *Introduction to Religion* (Harper &

Brothers, 1954); *Buddhism and Christianity: Some Bridges of Understanding* (The Westminster Press, 1962); *A Thousand Lives Away: Buddhism in Contemporary Burma* (Harvard University Press, 1965); and *In the Hope of Nibbana: An Essay on Theravada Buddhist Ethics* (The Open Court Publishing Company, 1964).

A few theologians studied with Whitehead. Nels Ferré developed a systematic theology that shows the stimulus of Whitehead's religious thought while insisting on a more transcendent view of God. During a period when antimetaphysical views prevailed, he helped to keep philosophical theology alive in such books as *The Christian Fellowship* (Harper & Brothers, 1940); *Return to Christianity* (Harper & Brothers, 1943); *Faith and Reason* (Harper & Brothers, 1946); *Evil and the Christian Faith* (Harper & Brothers, 1947); *The Christian Understanding of God* (Harper & Brothers, 1951); and *Christ and the Christian* (Harper & Brothers, 1958). More recently he has written *Reason in Religion* (Thomas Nelson & Sons, 1963); *The Living God of Nowhere and Nothing* (London: The Epworth Press, 1966; The Westminster Press, 1967); and *The Universal Word: A Theology for a Universal Faith* (The Westminster Press, 1969). Harvey Potthoff has not been as prolific as Ferré, but he has more closely associated himself with Whiteheadian theology. He recently published *God and the Celebration of Life* (Rand McNally & Company, 1969).

Two of Whitehead's students have devoted considerable attention to Whitehead's own thought. They are Victor Lowe and A. H. Johnson. Victor Lowe has taught for most of his career at Johns Hopkins University. He wrote an extended introduction to the book of essays on Whitehead edited by Paul A. Schilpp (see Section IV, below). This introduction, which provides an excellent intellectual biography, is greatly expanded with the inclusion of much systematic exposition in Lowe's full-length book, *Understanding Whitehead* (Johns Hopkins Press, 1962), which remains one of the best introductions to Whitehead's thought. A full-scale biography of Whitehead is being prepared by Lowe.

A. H. Johnson's teaching career has been in Canada at the University of Western Ontario. His two major writings on Whitehead's thought are *Whitehead's Theory of Reality* (Beacon Press, Inc., 1952) and *Whitehead's Philosophy of Civilization* (Beacon Press, Inc., 1958). He put together quotations from Whitehead in a book entitled *The Wit and Wisdom of Whitehead* (Beacon Press, Inc., 1947). He edited (and wrote an introduction to) a collection of Whitehead's essays under the title *The Interpretation of Science* (The Bobbs-Merrill Company, Inc., 1961). He also edited *American Essays in Social Philosophy* (Harper & Brothers, 1959).

III. CHARLES HARTSHORNE

One of Whitehead's assistants requires special attention here because of his decisive role in the emergence of process theology. This is Charles Hartshorne. He was never technically a student of Whitehead's, but after finishing his doctoral work he began in 1925 to hear Whitehead lecture and to grade papers for him. Hartshorne, like most of the others mentioned, was encouraged to continue the development of his own thought, which was already far advanced when he encountered Whitehead. (For one thing, he and Paul Weiss were editing the papers of Charles Peirce.) But his interests were such that he could appropriate many features of Whitehead's systematic position into his own. Like Weiss, he is recognized as a major figure in American philosophy. But, unlike Weiss, he has strongly identified the resulting philosophy with that of Whitehead, and through the years he has synthesized additional aspects of Whitehead's thought and even vocabulary into his own metaphysics. Further, Hartshorne's interests were strongly centered in the philosophy of religion and specifically in the understanding of God. This topic he developed far more fully than Whitehead. Also, from 1928 to 1955 he taught at the University of Chicago, strongly influencing the faculty and students in the Divinity School. The result has been that, in many respects, process theology has been as much Hartshornean as Whiteheadian.

Hartshorne's first book was *The Philosophy and Psychology of Sensation* (The University of Chicago Press, 1934), in which he argued (in agreement with Whitehead) against the absolute difference between so-called secondary and tertiary qualities, i.e., sensations and values. In *Beyond Humanism: Essays in the New Philosophy of Nature* (Willett, Clark & Company, 1937) he suggests that nature is lovable both as a whole (as God) and in its subhuman individual parts. *Man's Vision of God and the Logic of Theism* (Willett, Clark & Company, 1941) argues that the view of God as absolutely perfect in some respects and relatively perfect in others (so that God is surpassable by himself in a later state in these latter respects) is rationally as well as religiously superior to all other logical possibilities. *The Divine Relativity: A Social Conception of God* (Yale University Press, 1948) makes the same general point, arguing particularly against Thomism that God must be relative as well as absolute. Hartshorne and William L. Reese jointly wrote *Philosophers Speak of God* (The University of Chicago Press, 1953), which presents readings and commentary to show contrasting examples of modern panentheism (God as Eternal-Temporal

Consciousness, Knowing and Including the World in His Own Actuality [But Not in His Essence]), with examples of various other options. *Reality as Social Process: Studies in Metaphysics and Religion* (Beacon Press, Inc., 1953; reprinted with corrections, Hafner Publishing Co., Inc., 1971) probably provides the best opening into the way in which Hartshorne combines philosophical and religious interests in his understanding of God and the world. *The Logic of Perfection, and Other Essays in Neoclassical Metaphysics* (The Open Court Publishing Company, 1962) combines an extensive defense of the ontological argument with other essays, so that this book gives a quite complete overall picture of Hartshorne's philosophy. *Anselm's Discovery: A Re-examination of the Ontological Proof for God's Existence* (The Open Court Publishing Company, 1965) is what the subtitle indicates, plus a critical survey of responses to Anselm's argument. Hartshorne's interest in this abstract argument has seemed to distinguish his approach to God most clearly from that of Whitehead (see the second section of Chapter 3, above). But Hartshorne has stated that "All the arguments are phases of one 'global' argument, that *the properly formulated theistically religious view of life and reality is the most intelligible, self-consistent, and satisfactory one that can be conceived.* " This quotation is from p. 276 of Hartshorne's latest philosophical book, *Creative Synthesis and Philosophic Method* (La Salle, Ill.: The Open Court Publishing Company, 1970; London: SCM Press, Ltd., 1970), which provides a concise account of Hartshorne's mature convictions on most of the issues with which he has wrestled throughout his career. An adequate understanding of Hartshorne's views could be derived by reading it, perhaps along with his *Reality as Social Process.*

There are three other books in the Hartshornean corpus. *A Natural Theology for Our Time* (The Open Court Publishing Company, 1967) contains nothing new, but provides a brief and readable account of its topic. The publication of *Whitehead's Philosophy: Selected Essays, 1935–1970* (University of Nebraska Press, 1972) witnesses to the growing interest in Whitehead, and of Hartshorne's relation to him. *Born to Sing: An Interpretation and World Survey of Bird Song* (Indiana University Press, 1973) is the product of Hartshorne's second vocation, ornithology, and illustrates the way in which the aesthetic principles that are fundamental to Whitehead's and Hartshorne's philosophies can lead to fruitful scientific hypotheses.

There is also a body of secondary literature about Hartshorne. This overlaps extensively with the literature about Whitehead, but a few books dealing primarily with Hartshorne will be listed here. Eugene H. Peters, in *Hartshorne and Neoclassical Metaphysics: An Interpretation* (University of Nebraska Press, 1970), concentrates upon Hartshorne as metaphysician. Ralph E. James focused upon Hartshorne's theological relevance in *The Concrete God: A New Beginning for Theology—The Thought of Charles Hartshorne* (The Bobbs-Merrill Company, Inc., 1968). Recognition of Hartshorne's influence upon theology is reflected by the presence of Alan Gragg's *Charles Hartshorne* (Word Books, 1973) in the series "Makers of the Modern Theological Mind," edited by Robert E. Patterson. Religious interest in the comparison between Hartshorne and Whitehead is evidenced by the appearance of *Two Process Philosophers: Hartshorne's Encounter with Whitehead,* edited by Lewis S. Ford, in the American Academy of Religion series "AAR Studies in Religion" (No. 5, 1973). Several essays on Hartshorne are also included in *Charles Hartshorne and Henry Nelson Wieman,* Volume I of "Philosophy of Creativity Monograph Series" (Southern Illinois University, Central Publications, 1969). There has also been a Hartshorne Festschrift, *Process and Divinity,* ed. by William L. Reese and Eugene Freeman (The Open Court Publishing Company, 1964). It contains a few articles dealing directly with Hartshorne's thought.

The Festschrift also contains a bibliography of Hartshorne's writings to 1963. A bibliography of his writings to 1967 is found in Ralph James's book, *The Concrete God,* mentioned above. Alan Gragg's book, *Charles Hartshorne,* also cited above, contains a selective bibliography that includes more recent publications. A primary bibliography to 1975 is contained in *Process Studies,* Vol. 6, No. 1 (Spring 1976). A secondary bibliography on Hartshorne can be found in *Process Studies,* Vol. 3, No. 3 (Fall 1973), with dissertations listed in Vol. 3, No. 4 (Winter 1973).

IV. WHITEHEAD'S EARLY
PHILOSOPHICAL RECEPTION

Generally speaking, the more rigorous study of Whitehead's philosophy began in 1958. However, there were several books devoted to his thought prior to that time. In America, there appeared: N. P. Stallknecht, *Studies in the Philosophy of Creation, with Especial Reference to Bergson and Whitehead* (Princeton University Press, 1934); Edmund J. Thompson, *An Analysis of the Thought of Alfred North Whitehead and William Ernest Hocking Concerning Good and Evil* (University of Chicago, 1935); F. C. Ward, "Mind in Whitehead's Philosophy" (dissertation, Yale University, 1937); D. L. Miller and G. V. Gentry, *The Philosophy of*

A. N. Whitehead (Burgess Publishing Company, 1938); E. P. Shahan, *Whitehead's Theory of Experience* (King's Crown Press, 1950); L. A. Foley, *A Critique of the Philosophy of Being of Alfred North Whitehead in the Light of Thomistic Philosophy* (The Catholic University of America Press, 1946); W. W. Hammerschmidt, *Whitehead's Philosophy of Time* (King's Crown Press, 1947); and H. K. Wells's critical study from a Hegelian viewpoint, *Process and Unreality* (King's Crown Press, 1950; Gordian Press, Inc., 1975). The critical study from this period which has attracted the most attention is John W. Blyth, *Whitehead's Theory of Knowledge* (Brown University, 1941). Blyth argued that Whitehead's epistemology is fundamentally inconsistent, since his reference to "mutual prehensions" seems to contradict his insistence that there are no causal relations between contemporaries.

Two books with some helpful essays on Whitehead's philosophy were also published during this period. *The Philosophy of Alfred North Whitehead*, edited by Paul A. Schilpp (Northwestern University, 1941; 2d ed., Tudor Publishing Company, 1951), appeared in the series "Library of Living Philosophers." Victor Lowe, Charles Hartshorne, and A. H. Johnson contributed the three essays contained in *Whitehead and the Modern World* (Beacon Press, Inc., 1950).

Although what Whitehead wrote after leaving Great Britain received its major response in America, several books on his later thought were published in England. Dorothy Emmet wrote the useful book, *Whitehead's Philosophy of Organism* (London: Macmillan & Co., Ltd., 1932; 2d ed., New York: St. Martin's Press, 1966). Her later study, *The Nature of Metaphysical Thinking* (London: Macmillan & Co., Ltd., 1945), shows the influence of Whitehead. Other books were Rashvihari Das, *The Philosophy of Whitehead* (London: James Clarke & Co., Ltd., 1938; New York: Russell & Russell Inc., 1964), and A. K. Sarkar, *An Outline of Whitehead's Philosophy* (London: Stockwell, 1940). R. G. Collingwood's *The Idea of Nature* (Oxford University Press, 1945) reflects significant influence from Whitehead.

A few books also were published in other countries during this period. In France there were M. A. Bera's *A. N. Whitehead: Un philosophe de l'expérience* (Paris: Hermann, 1948) and F. Cesselin's *La Philosophie organique de Whitehead* (Paris: Presses Universitaires de France, 1952). In Italy there was C. Orsi's *La filosofia dell'organismo di A. N. Whitehead* (Naples: Libreria Scientifica, 1956). In Japan, S. Ichii wrote *Whitehead no Tetsugaku* ("The Philosophy of Whitehead") (Tokyo: Kobundo, 1956). And in India there was published J. N. Mohanty's *Nicolai Hartmann and*

Alfred North Whitehead: A Study in Recent Platonism (Calcutta: Progressive Publishers, 1957).

V. WHITEHEAD'S RECENT
PHILOSOPHICAL RECEPTION

In the late 1950's more detailed studies of Whitehead began to appear. In 1956, Nathaniel Lawrence contributed his careful study, *Whitehead's Philosophical Development: A Critical History of the Background of Process and Reality* (University of California Press). However, he stopped short of *Process and Reality*. Ivor Leclerc broke this barrier with his analysis of Whitehead's systematic position: *Whitehead's Metaphysics: An Introductory Exposition* (New York: The Macmillan Company, 1958; London: George Allen & Unwin, Ltd, 1958). It explained Whitehead's distinctive position in relation to the history of metaphysical discussion, especially that of the Greeks. The following year William Christian published what is still the most detailed inquiry into the meaning of Whitehead's basic ideas, *An Interpretation of Whitehead's Metaphysics* (Yale University Press, 1959). And in 1962, Victor Lowe's previously mentioned *Understanding Whitehead* appeared.

The availability of this excellent secondary literature has been essential to raising the level of discussion of Whitehead to precision, since even today few philosophers can read *Process and Reality* on their own without bewilderment if not exasperation. This situation has been ameliorated even further by the appearance of *A Key to Whitehead's Process and Reality* (The Macmillan Company, 1966), prepared by Donald W. Sherburne. This book is largely in Whitehead's own words, but (unlike *Process and Reality* itself) introduces his major ideas topically. Three collections of essays reflect the new level of the discussion: *The Relevance of Whitehead: Philosophical Essays in Commemoration of the Centenary of the Birth of Alfred North Whitehead*, edited by Ivor Leclerc (New York: The Macmillan Company, 1961; London: George Allen & Unwin, Ltd., 1961); *Alfred North Whitehead: Essays on His Philosophy* (Prentice-Hall, Inc., 1963), edited by George Kline; and *Studies in Whitehead's Philosophy*, which appeared as Volume 10 of *Tulane Studies in Philosophy* (Tulane University, 1961). (More recently, Volumes 23 [1974] and 24 [1975] of this same journal have been entitled *Studies in Process Philosophy* I and II.)

Books manifesting the new level of precision to varying degrees include Paul F. Schmidt, *Perception and Cosmology in Whitehead's Philosophy* (Rutgers University Press, 1967); Jude D. Weisenbeck, *Alfred North*

Whitehead's Philosophy of Values (Mount St. Paul College, 1969); J. W. Lango, *Whitehead's Ontology* (State University of New York Press, 1972); and Nathaniel Lawrence, *Alfred North Whitehead: A Primer of His Philosophy* (Twayne Publishers, 1974). One of the more important books in recent years is Richard M. Martin, *Whitehead's Categoreal Scheme and Other Papers* (The Hague: Martinus Nijhoff, 1974). A book designed to express the spirit and insight of Whitehead is C. R. Eisendrath, *The Unifying Moment: The Psychological Philosophy of William James and Alfred North Whitehead* (Harvard University Press, 1971).

A sustained criticism, which has evoked considerable discussion, is Edward Pols's *Whitehead's Metaphysics: A Critical Examination of Process and Reality* (Southern Illinois University Press, 1967). Pols argues that Whitehead's philosophy, despite its intention, does not really provide a consistent basis for affirming human freedom. Discussions of Pols's thesis, along with many other important articles, are found in the "Special Issue on Whitehead" of *The Southern Journal of Philosophy,* Vol. 7, No. 4 (Winter 1969–70).

This special issue was edited by Lewis S. Ford, who also edited the previously mentioned *Two Process Philosophers: Hartshorne's Encounter with Whitehead.* Ford has made one of his major contributions to the development of process thought in the role of editor, in that he is also the literary editor of the journal *Process Studies* (of which John B. Cobb, Jr., is a coeditor). This journal, which was begun in 1971, is primarily devoted to the evaluation and employment of Whiteheadian process thought. Besides many articles, it contains books reviews (including reviews of several of the books mentioned here) and abstracts of relevant articles appearing in other journals. Ford has also contributed directly to the ongoing technical discussion of process thought through several essays in philosophical and theological journals.

Whitehead is treated in some histories of philosophy. Of these, one is especially worthy of mention, in that it not only has a lengthy and sophisticated treatment of Whitehead, but is also written from a largely Whiteheadian perspective. This is Albert W. Levi's *Philosophy and the Modern World* (Indiana University Press, 1959).

While the recent growth in interest in Whiteheadian studies occurred primarily in the United States, a few books have been published in other countries in recent years. In England, Wolfe Mays wrote *The Philosophy of Whitehead* (New York: The Macmillan Company, 1959; London: George Allen & Unwin, Ltd., 1959). And Martin Jordan published *New Shapes of Reality: Aspects of A. N. Whitehead's Philosophy* (London:

George Allen & Unwin, Ltd., 1968). Italy saw the appearance of E. Paci's *La filosofia di Whitehead e i problemi del tempo e della struttura* (Milan: Goliardica, 1965), and C. Sini's *Whitehead e la funzione della filosofia* (Padua: Marsilio, 1965). One of the most careful and thorough examinations of Whitehead's philosophy appeared in France: *La Philosophie de Whitehead et le problème de Dieu* (Paris: Beauchesne, 1968), by Alix Parmentier, of Fribourg, Switzerland. In Germany a dissertation was produced, K. Heipcke's "Die Philosophie des Ereignisses bei Alfred North Whitehead" (Würzburg, 1964). In Spain there appeared *La filosofia de Alfred North Whitehead* (Madrid: Editorial Tecnos, 1967), by Jorge Enjuto-Bernal of the University of Puerto Rico, and *Lo individual y su relación interna en Alfred North Whitehead* (Universidad de Navarra, 1977), by F. A. Simonpietri, also of the University of Puerto Rico. In India, L. V. Rajagopal has written *The Philosophy of A. N. Whitehead: The Concept of Reality and Organism* (University of Mysore, 1966).

VI. WHITEHEAD'S INFLUENCE ON OTHER DISCIPLINES

One major attraction of Whitehead is that his thought seems to offer a way in which the disparate branches of modern learning can be reintegrated. This potential has been recognized and appreciated among the small group working on the relation of science and religion. The following books indicate that Whitehead has an important following here: L. Charles Birch, *Nature and God* (The Westminster Press, 1965); Kenneth Cauthen, *Science, Secularization and God: Toward a Theology of the Future* (Abingdon Press, 1969); Ian Barbour, *Issues in Science and Religion* (Prentice-Hall, Inc., 1966); Harold K. Schilling, *The New Consciousness in Science and Religion* (United Church Press, A Pilgrim Press Book, 1973). Although we will see that Langdon Gilkey is a critic of process theology, he appeals to Whitehead in relating science and religion, as in *Religion and the Scientific Future: Reflections on Myth, Science, and Theology* (Harper & Row, Publishers, Inc., 1970).

Some work has been done on Whitehead's philosophy of science. Laurence Bright wrote a little book called *Whitehead's Philosophy of Science* (Sheed & Ward, Inc., 1960), and Robert M. Palter published a much more technical study in the same year: *Whitehead's Philosophy of Science* (Chicago: The University of Chicago Press; and London: Cambridge University Press, 1960; 2d corrected impression, The University of Chicago Press, 1970). J. M. Burgers published *Experience and Conceptual Activity:*

A Philosophical Essay Based Upon the Writings of A. N. Whitehead (M.I.T. Press, 1965). Milič Čapek's book *The Philosophical Impact of Contemporary Physics* (D. Van Nostrand Company, Inc., 1961) is heavily Whiteheadian. Ivor Leclerc shows Whitehead's important contribution to the philosophy of nature in *The Nature of Physical Existence* (London: George Allen & Unwin, Ltd., 1972; New York: Humanities Press, 1972).

In the field of physics Whitehead's theory of relativity has been examined by J. L. Synge in *The Relativity Theory of A. N. Whitehead* (University of Maryland, 1951). David Bohm has read Whitehead and recognizes his influence in his work in quantum theory. Bohm's writings include *Causality and Chance in Modern Physics* (D. Van Nostrand Company, Inc., 1957; University of Pennsylvania Press, 1971) and an extensive contribution to the volumes edited by C. H. Waddington, mentioned below.

The Australian biologist W. E. Agar saw the implications of Whitehead for his field and expressed them in *A Contribution to the Theory of the Living Organism* (Melbourne: Melbourne University Press, 1943). His student L. Charles Birch shared Agar's enthusiasm and has published his views in a number of articles as well as in the book already mentioned, *Nature and God*. Richard Overman makes a Whiteheadian contribution to the interpretation of evolution in *Evolution and the Christian Doctrine of Creation* (The Westminster Press, 1967). C. H. Waddington has felt the influence of Whitehead throughout his career. This is reflected in the two volumes he edited, *Towards a Theoretical Biology* (Edinburgh University Press, Vol I, 1968; Vol. II, 1969). A meeting of scientists and philosophers interested in Whitehead, including many of those mentioned above, was held in Bellagio, Italy, in June 1974, and it is hoped that the papers from this conference, focusing chiefly on biology, will be published under the title *Mind in Nature*. This conference was sponsored by the Center for Process Studies (located in Claremont, California), which hopes to stimulate exploration of the possible fruitfulness of Whitehead's theories in various areas, such as the natural and social sciences, where thus far little work has been done.

Several dissertations and journal articles have been written on Whitehead's educational views, and the implications of his thought for the philosophy of education. Books published in this area include H. W. Holmes, *The Educational Views of Alfred North Whitehead* (Harvard University Graduate School of Education, 1943); Bernard E. Meland, *Higher Education and the Human Spirit* (The University of Chicago Press, 1953); F. C. Wegener, *The Organic Philosophy of Education* (W. C. Brown Company, 1957); H. B. Dunkel, *Whitehead on Education* (Ohio State

University Press, 1965); and F. Cafaro, *Il pensiero educativo di A. N. Whitehead* (Bologna: Leonardi, 1969).

Whitehead's relevance for other areas of thought has also begun to be explored. In aesthetics, there is Donald Sherburne's *A Whiteheadian Aesthetic: Some Implications of Whitehead's Metaphysical Speculation* (Yale University Press, 1961); C. H. Waddington's *Behind Appearance: A Study of the Relations Between Painting and the Natural Sciences in this Century* (Edinburgh University Press, 1969; Cambridge, Mass.: The MIT Press, 1970); and F. David Martin's *Art and the Religious Experience: The Language of the Sacred* (Bucknell University Press, 1972).

William Widick Schroeder has applied process thought to the sociology of religion in *Cognitive Structures and Religious Research* (Michigan State University Press, 1971). In 1949 Samuel H. Beer provided a Whiteheadian theory of government in *The City of Reason* (Harvard University Press). David L. Hall has contributed *The Civilization of Experience: A Whiteheadian Theory of Culture* (Fordham University Press, 1973). Granville C. Henry, Jr., has given extended attention to Whitehead's mathematics in *Logos: Mathematics and Christian Theology* (Bucknell University Press, 1976).

Worthy of special mention is Ervin Laszlo, who has published in more than one country and has related Whitehead's thought to general systems theory. His books include: *Essential Society: An Ontological Reconstruction* (The Hague: Martinus Nijhoff, 1963); *Beyond Scepticism and Realism: A Constructive Exploration of Husserlian and Whiteheadian Methods of Inquiry* (The Hague: Martinus Nijhoff, 1966); *System, Structure, and Experience: Toward a Scientific Theory of Mind* (Gordon and Breach, 1969); *La métaphysique de Whitehead* (The Hague: Martinus Nijhoff, 1970); *Introduction to Systems Philosophy: Toward a New Paradigm of Contemporary Thought* (Gordon and Breach, 1972); and *The Systems View of the World: The Natural Philosophy of the New Developments in the Sciences* (George Braziller, Inc., 1972). Laszlo believes that Whitehead's philosophy of organism can best be updated in the light of more recent scientific research by replacing the notion of "organism" with that of a self-sustaining "system."

Another attractive feature of Whitehead to theologians working in our pluralistic age is the extent to which his thought transcends the usual limits of Western philosophy. This has been appreciatively recognized by a number of Eastern commentators, and the potential for intercultural and interreligious understanding that Whitehead offers is now beginning to be realized. F. S. C. Northrop's book *The Meeting of East and West* has already been mentioned. Mary Wyman, in *The Lure for Feeling: In the Creative Process* (Philosophical Library, Inc., 1960), explored the affinities of Whitehead's thought to that of China, in particular to Taoism. A number of articles have been published on the relation of Whitehead to Buddhist philosophy, and the October 1975 issue of *Philosophy East and West* (Vol. 25, No. 4) is devoted to this subject. A. K. Sarkar has recently written *Whitehead's Four Principles from West-East Perspectives* (Patna: Bharati Bhawan, 1974). From the Hindu side, Satya Prakash Singh has written *Sri Aurobindo and Whitehead on the Nature of God* (Aligarh: Vigyan Prakashan, 1972), and S. K. Mitra has a chapter on Aurobindo and Whitehead in his book *The Meeting of the East and the West in Sri Aurobindo's Philosophy* (Sri Aurobindo Ashram Press, 1968).

VII. PROCESS THEOLOGY: THE CHICAGO SCHOOL

The major center of theological receptivity to Whitehead's influence was the Divinity School of the University of Chicago. Indeed, process theology can trace its history almost as well through this school as to Whitehead. What is today called process theology is largely the result of the way Whitehead's influence, along with the teaching of Charles Harts-horne, modified the thought of members of this school. Accordingly, we offer a brief guide to the history of this school with special reference to selected representatives and their major writings.

The history begins with the move to Chicago in 1892 of the faculty of the Baptist Union Theological Seminary to become the nucleus of the new university faculty. Two years later Shailer Mathews came to teach New Testament history and, later, theology. As teacher, writer, churchman, and dean, he was a dominant figure in shaping the school until his retirement in 1933. He understood Christianity as a sociohistorical movement with changing beliefs, and he opposed the effort to find a constant kernel within it. The sociohistorical method reveals the character of Christianity and illumines the superstructure of beliefs that the movement has produced. Mathews applied this method to the study of Christianity in such books as: *The Social Teaching of Jesus* (The Macmillan Company, 1897); *A History of New Testament Times in Palestine* (London: Macmillan & Co., Ltd., 1899); *The Spiritual Interpretation of History* (Harvard University Press, 1916); *The Atonement and the Social Process* (The Macmillan Company, 1930); and *Christianity and Social Process* (Harper & Brothers, 1934).

Mathews recognized that his method presented Christianity in a highly relativistic way. He did not believe, however, that this meant that normative theological inquiry was superseded. On the contrary, he held that the theological task is to formulate ideas about reality in that way which will both further the concern of the movement founded by Jesus and be appropriate to what is known about the world through the sciences. He edited *Contributions of Science to Religion* (D. Appleton and Company, 1927); and he discussed the beliefs now appropriate to Christians in such books as: *The Growth of the Idea of God* (The Macmillan Company, 1931) and *Is God Emeritus?* (The Macmillan Company, 1940).

A younger colleague of Mathews was Shirley Jackson Case, who developed the sociohistorical method with still greater thoroughness. His first book was *The Evolution of Early Christianity: A Genetic Study of First-Century Christianity in Relation to its Religious Environment* (The University of Chicago Press, 1914). Important later works included: *The Social Origins of Christianity* (The University of Chicago Press, 1923); *Jesus, A New Biography* (The University of Chicago Press, 1927); *Experience with the Supernatural in Early Christian Times* (The Century Company, 1929); and *The Social Triumph of the Ancient Church* (Harper & Brothers, 1933).

In 1926, shortly after the publication of Whitehead's *Religion in the Making,* the Chicago faculty invited Henry Nelson Wieman to come for a lecture to explain this book. They had long admired Whitehead but were troubled by the apparently speculative character of his treatment of religion. Wieman's success in this assignment paved the way for his invitation to join the faculty in the following year. His influence there during the next twenty years shifted the main focus of the school from sociohistorical studies to philosophy of religion. At first this meant for Wieman the reflective, empirical study of religious experience as a dimension of all experience. This was reflected in such books as *Religious Experience and Scientific Method* (The Macmillan Company, 1926); *The Wrestle of Religion with Truth* (The Macmillan Company, 1927); and *Now We Must Choose* (The Macmillan Company, 1941). The second of these included two chapters exploring Whitehead's writings.

In Wieman's middle period the focus shifted from religious experience to the examination of that process through which human good grows. He analyzed this process in detail, showing that it cannot be controlled and manipulated but only served. He called for complete devotion to this process, and he named the process God. He worked out this position in such books as *The Source of Human Good* (The University of Chicago Press, 1946), *The Directive in History* (Beacon Press, Inc., 1949), and *Man's Ultimate Commitment* (Southern Illinois University Press, 1958).

In later years Wieman distanced himself more from both Christianity and the philosophy of Whitehead, urging the importance of releasing the process of creative good to full effectiveness without concern for labels and philosophical speculation. This position is vigorously pressed in such books as *Intellectual Foundation of Faith* (Philosophical Library, Inc., 1961), and *Religious Inquiry: Some Explorations* (Beacon Press, Inc., 1968). A bibliography of Wieman's writings and of writings about him is to be found in *The Empirical Theology of Henry Nelson Wieman,* edited by Robert W. Bretall (The Macmillan Company, 1963). There is a supplement in *Seeking a Faith for a New Age,* edited by Cedric L. Hepler (Scarecrow Press, Inc., 1975).

However, Wieman during his middle period had encouraged his students both to read Whitehead and to work through their positions in relation to the history of Christian thought. Daniel Day Williams was particularly successful in moving in both of these directions. He taught at Chicago, and after 1955 at Union Theological Seminary until his untimely death in 1973. He functioned as the senior statesman of process theology. His major works are *What Present-Day Theologians Are Thinking* (3d revised ed., Harper & Row, Publishers, Inc., 1967); *God's Grace and Man's Hope* (Harper & Brothers, 1949); and *The Spirit and the Forms of Love* (Harper & Row, Publishers, Inc., 1968). The latter two books constitute the most fully developed theological statements of the movement. A bibliography of Williams' writings can be found in the Winter-Summer 1975 issue (Vol. 30, Nos. 2–4) of the *Union Seminary Quarterly Review,* which is a Festschrift in his honor.

Bernard Loomer has published very little, but through his leadership as dean of the Divinity School of the University of Chicago from 1945 to 1954 and his teaching (now at the Graduate Theological Union in Berkeley, California) he has played and continues to play an important role. One of his articles, "Christian Faith and Process Philosophy" (*Journal of Religion,* Vol. 29, No. 3 [1949], pp. 181–203), was an early milestone in the development of process theology. An excerpt from his influential dissertation, "The Theological Significance of the Method of Empirical Analysis in the Philosophy of A. N. Whitehead" (University of Chicago, 1942), has been published as "Whitehead's Method of Empirical Analysis" in *Process Theology: Basic Writings* (Paulist/Newman Press, 1971), edited by Ewert H. Cousins.

Another key figure in the Chicago school, less closely associated with the influence of Whitehead, has been Bernard Meland. He drew upon the wider currents of American philosophical and religious thought as a basis for understanding the historic themes of Christian faith. He particularly stressed the importance of "appreciative awareness" and its relevance to the study of the Christian myth. Among his important systematic books are *Seeds of Redemption* (The Macmillan Company, 1947); *America's Spiritual Culture* (Harper & Brothers, 1948); *Faith and Culture* (Toronto: Oxford University Press, 1953; London: George Allen & Unwin, Ltd., 1955); *The Realities of Faith* (Oxford University Press, 1962); *The Secularization of Modern Cultures* (Oxford University Press, 1966); and *Fallible Forms and Symbols: Discourses on Method for a Theology of Culture* (Fortress Press, 1976). A primary-secondary bibliography of Meland's writings is contained in *Process Studies,* Vol. 5, No. 4 (Winter, 1975).

Meland has also been the historian and interpreter of the Chicago school. He edited a volume of papers by members of that school entitled *The Future of Empirical Theology* (The University of Chicago Press, 1969), and his introduction to that volume is the best study of the school as a whole. Many of the major figures in the school are also presented at greater length in Randolph Crump Miller, *The Spirit of American Theology* (United Church Press, A Pilgrim Press Book, 1974).

Although the University of Chicago is no longer the leading center of process theology, alumni are continuing the tradition elsewhere. Schubert M. Ogden has taught at Perkins School of Theology of Southern Methodist University with a short interim at the Divinity School of the University of Chicago. He has established himself as a leader in process theology through lectures, articles, and two major books. The first of these, *Christ Without Myth* (Harper & Row, Publishers, Inc., 1961), was a critique of Rudolf Bultmann for failing to carry his program of demythologizing through to the end. Ogden argued that what is re-presented in Christ is man's primordial possibility for responding to God's love, available to all. In his second book, *The Reality of God, and Other Essays* (Harper & Row, Publishers, Inc., 1966), Ogden developed a sustained argument for the existence of God as the ground of secularity. In these books Ogden has developed the theological implications especially of the philosophy of Charles Hartshorne. He stresses that the very belief that life is meaningful points to a prereflective faith in the kind of God that Hartshorne's philosophy explicates.

Another Chicago alumnus, John B. Cobb, Jr., has taught chiefly at the School of Theology at Claremont, California. He made systematic use of Whitehead's conceptuality in *A Christian Natural Theology: Based on the Thought of Alfred North Whitehead* (The Westminster Press, 1965). Cobb's subsequent writings have attempted to speak from the

Whiteheadian perspective on contemporary theological questions without employing the technical philosophical vocabulary. These include *The Structure of Christian Existence* (The Westminster Press, 1967) (some of its leading ideas are reflected in Chapter 5, above); *God and the World* (The Westminster Press, 1969); *Is It Too Late? A Theology of Ecology* (Bruce, 1972); *Liberal Christianity at the Crossroads* (The Westminster Press, 1973); and *Christ in a Pluralistic Age* (The Westminster Press, 1975) (some of its ideas are reflected in Chapter 6, above).

William A. Beardslee, whose work at Chicago was chiefly in New Testament, has published (in addition to articles relating process thought to New Testament scholarship) *A House for Hope: A Study in Process and Biblical Thought* (The Westminster Press, 1972). This book relates process philosophy both to the New Testament and to central theological themes.

VIII. PROCESS THEOLOGY:
OTHER INFLUENCES AND RECENT WRITINGS

In addition to his influence on his own students and his influence on the Chicago school, Whitehead had some early influence on theology. In England, William Temple found certain aspects of Whitehead's thought congenial, as reflected in *Nature, Man and God* (London: Macmillan & Co., Ltd., 1935). And Lionel Thornton explicitly used some of Whitehead's philosophical ideas, especially regarding evolution, in *The Incarnate Lord* (London: Longmans, Green and Co., Ltd., 1928). However, this book, which was written prior to the appearance of *Process and Reality,* is not a Whiteheadian Christology so much as a supernaturalistic Christology imposed upon an evolutionary context. H. Richard Niebuhr was somewhat influenced by Whitehead, as indicated in *The Meaning of Revelation* (The Macmillan Company, 1941); but his philosophical framework was basically Kantian. Although this fact was not widely recognized, the thought of his brother, Reinhold Niebuhr, was more compatible with and probably more influenced by Whitehead's thought.

When considering the influence of Whitehead on theology outside the Chicago school during this period, the name of W. Norman Pittenger stands out. He brought to his study of Whitehead the sensitivities of a Canadian Anglican steeped in church history. In 1959, Pittenger produced the first genuinely Whiteheadian Christology, *The Word Incarnate: A Study of the Doctrine of the Person of Christ* (Harper & Brothers). Since then he has written over a dozen books showing Whitehead's relevance to Christian theology. Two of his books, *Process Thought and Christian Faith*

(The Macmillan Company, 1968) and *Alfred North Whitehead* (John Knox Press, 1969), provide good introductions to the general significance of process philosophy for Christian faith. Pittenger has entered into more explicitly Christian themes in *God in Process* (London: SCM Press, 1967); *God's Way with Men: A Study of the Relationship Between God and Man in Providence, "Miracle," and Prayer* (London: Hodder & Stoughton, Ltd., 1969; Valley Forge, Pa.: Judson Press, 1970); *"The Last Things" in a Process Perspective* (London: Epworth Press, 1970); and *The Holy Spirit* (United Church Press, A Pilgrim Press Book, 1974). He has given special attention to sexuality in *Making Sexuality Human* (United Church Press, A Pilgrim Press Book, 1970); *Time for Consent: A Christian's Approach to Homosexuality* (London: SCM Press, 2d ed., revised, 1970); and *Love and Control in Sexuality* (United Church Press, A Pilgrim Press Book, 1974). He has related his Christological reflections to recent debates in *Christology Reconsidered* (London: SCM Press, 1970).

After teaching at General Theological Seminary in New York for many years, Pittenger began teaching at Cambridge University, introducing British colleagues and students to the thought of the Englishman Whitehead. Peter Hamilton's *The Living God and the Modern World* (London: Hodder & Stoughton, Ltd., 1967) gives evidence of Pittenger's influence in England even before he moved there. Hamilton's is the first definitely Whiteheadian theological book to be published by a British thinker.

Other British theologians show the influence of Pittenger and thus of process theology. Most important of these is John A. T. Robinson, whose treatment of God changed markedly from *Honest to God* (The Westminster Press, 1963), his most widely read work, to *Exploration Into God* (Stanford University Press, 1967). In this latter work there is fully recognized indebtedness to process theology. The influence appears also in *The Human Face of God* (The Westminster Press, 1973). David A. Pailin has not yet produced a book in this area, but through his articles he has emerged as one of Great Britain's leading interpreters of process thought.

Most of the earlier Catholic responses to Whitehead and process theology were critical. The chapter on Whitehead in *He Who Is* (London: Longmans, Green & Company, Inc., 1943), by the Anglo-Catholic Thomist, E. L. Mascall, is representative of this critical rejection. The attitude of Leonard J. Eslick, who wrote articles on Whitehead (e.g., "Substance, Change and Causality in Whitehead," *Philosophy and Phenomenological Research,* Vol. 18 [1958], pp. 503–513; "God in the Metaphysics of Whitehead," in *New Themes in Christian Philosophy,* ed. by R. M. McInerny [University of Notre Dame Press, 1968]) and introduced Whitehead to his students at St. Louis University, could be described as critically receptive. James W. Felt, who is now preparing a book, reflects Eslick's influence but also typifies the greater interest in Whitehead in the current generation of Catholic thinkers. Walter Stokes, who taught at Fordham University, was the first Catholic theologian to write quite positively about Whitehead's metaphysical theism. He introduced Whitehead into Thomistic theological circles, but died before producing a full-scale treatment. His many valuable articles include "Freedom as Perfection: Whitehead, Thomas and Augustine," *Proceedings of the American Catholic Philosophic Association,* Vol. 36 (1962), pp. 134–142, and "Whitehead's Challenge to Theistic Realism," *New Scholasticism,* Vol. 38 (1964), pp. 1–21. Today Ewert Cousins of Fordham represents the increasingly favorable attitude toward Whitehead among Catholic theologians, and also the fact that this greater receptiveness is due in part to the influence of Teilhard de Chardin. Cousins, who is president of the American Teilhard de Chardin Association, included materials from both Whiteheadian and Teilhardian sources in the book he edited entitled *Process Theology: Basic Writings* (Paulist/Newman Press, 1971). Cousins was also the central figure responsible for a conference that brought together representatives from these two movements, along with some "theologians of hope." The papers from this conference appear in *Hope and the Future of Man* (Fortress Press, 1972), which Cousins edited. David Tracy of the Divinity School of the University of Chicago, who has done considerable work with Bernard Lonergan's thought, has become increasingly favorable to process theology, as evidenced by his review article "God's Reality: The Most Important Issue," *National Catholic Reporter,* July 23, 1972, and *Anglican Theological Review,* Vol. 55, No. 2 (April 1973), pp. 218–224, and *Blessed Rage for Order: The New Pluralism in Theology* (Seabury Press, 1975). Charles Winquist has used Whitehead in *The Transcendental Imagination* (The Hague: Martinus Nijhoff, 1972) and *The Communion of Possibility* (New Horizons Press, 1975). The first two specifically Whiteheadian Catholic theological books are Bernard M. Lee, *The Becoming of the Church: A Process Theology of the Structure of Christian Experience* (Paulist/Newman Press, 1974), and the introductory work by Robert B. Mellert, *What Is Process Theology?* (Paulist/Newman Press, 1975).

Several books in process theology by Protestants have appeared in the last ten years, many of which are directly or indirectly products of the Chicago school. Richard Overman's book, *Evolution and the Christian Doctrine of Creation,* has already been mentioned. Don S. Browning, whose recent treatment of Erik Erikson has received much attention, wrote in 1966 a Whiteheadian-Hartshornean study entitled *Atonement and Psychotherapy* (The Westminster Press). Eugene H. Peters has provided in *The Creative Advance* what its subtitle says: *An Introduction to Process Philosophy as a Context for Christian Faith* (The Bethany Press, 1966). William D. Dean has called for a deeper religious appreciation of the primacy of the aesthetic dimensions in Whitehead's thought in *Coming To: A Theology of Beauty* (The Westminster Press, 1972) and has offered an exposition of "aesthetic love" in *Love Before the Fall* (The Westminster Press, 1976). David Ray Griffin produced a treatment of Jesus as the decisive revelation of God in *A Process Christology* (The Westminster Press, 1973). He is also publishing a full-scale Whiteheadian treatment of the problem of evil as *God, Power, and Evil: A Process Theodicy* (The Westminster Press, 1976). Some of its ideas are reflected in Chapter 4, above.

In philosophy of religion and philosophical theology from a Whiteheadian perspective, Bowman Clarke published *Language and Natural Theology* (The Hague: Mouton & Co., 1966; New York: Humanities Press, Inc., 1967); C. J. Curtis wrote *The Task of Philosophical Theology* (Philosophical Library, Inc., 1967); and Kenneth F. Thompson, Jr., has published a full-scale treatment in *Whitehead's Philosophy of Religion* (The Hague: Mouton & Co., 1971; New York: Humanities Press, Inc., 1971). Frederick Ferré has shown his friendliness to process thought in *Language, Logic and God* (New York: Harper & Brothers, 1961, 1969; London: Eyre & Spottiswoode, Ltd., 1962; London: William Collins Sons & Co., Ltd., 1970) and *Basic Modern Philosophy of Religion* (New York: Charles Scribner's Sons, 1967; London: George Allen & Unwin, Ltd., 1968).

Lyman Lundeen has elaborated a Whiteheadian hermeneutic in *Risk and Rhetoric in Religion* (Fortress Press, 1972), and William Beardslee and Kent H. Richards are giving leadership to further work in this field.

A number of more popular theological writings are closely associated with process theology. These include J. Edward Carothers, *The Pusher and the Puller: A Concept of God* (Abingdon Press, 1968); Louis Cassels, *The Reality of God* (Doubleday & Company, Inc., 1971); and George W. Cornell, *The Untamed God* (Harper & Row, Publishers, Inc., 1975).

The growth of interest in ecology served to stimulate further interest in Whitehead's thought and its relevance to theology. John B. Cobb, Jr.'s little book *Is It Too Late? A Theology of Ecology* has been mentioned. Other books that reflect a heavy influence from Whitehead are Henlee H. Barnette, *The Church and the Ecological Crisis* (Wm. B. Eerdmans Company, 1972); *Technology—The God That Failed* (The Westminster Press, 1971), by Dorothy M. Slusser and Gerald H. Slusser; Kenneth Cauthen, *Christian Biopolitics: A Credo and Strategy for the Future* (Abingdon Press, 1971); Eric C. Rust, *Nature—Garden or Desert? An Essay in Environmental Theology* (Word Books, 1971). Ian Barbour has written one book in this area, *Science and Secularity: The Ethics of Technology* (Harper & Row, Publishers, Inc., 1970), and edited two others: *Earth Might Be Fair: Reflections on Ethics, Religion, and Ecology* (Prentice-Hall, Inc., 1972) and *Western Man and Environmental Ethics* (Addison-Wesley Publishing Company, 1973).

There are numerous criticisms of process theology, and especially of Whitehead's doctrine of God. E. L. Mascall's *He Who Is* has already been mentioned. Stephen L. Ely, in *The Religious Availability of Whitehead's God: A Critical Analysis* (University of Wisconsin Press, 1942), argued that this God is not religiously available, because he is not all-powerful, and because the priority of the aesthetic means that God is not morally perfect. Langdon Gilkey, in *Maker of Heaven and Earth: A Study of the Christian Doctrine of Creation* (Doubleday & Company, Inc., 1959), argued that a more transcendent deity is required than that of Whitehead. More recently, Robert C. Neville, in *God the Creator: On the Transcendence and Presence of God* (Chicago: The University of Chicago Press, 1968; Toronto: The University of Toronto Press, 1968), has reemphasized this criticism in careful analyses of Whitehead and Hartshorne. In *Evil and the Concept of God* (Charles C Thomas, Publishers, 1968), Edward H. Madden and Peter H. Hare argue that process theology is shipwrecked on the problem of evil. Cornelio Fabro, who virtually identifies "theism" with the Thomistic understanding of God, treats Whitehead's philosophy as a version of modern atheism in *Introduzione all'ateismo moderno* (Rome: Editrice Studium, 1964), translated as *God in Exile: Modern Atheism,* tr. by Arthur Gibson (Paulist/Newman Press, 1968).

There are now several collections of essays in process theology. Ewert Cousins' *Process Theology: Basic Writings* has already been mentioned. The other major collection is *Process Philosophy and Christian Thought* (The Bobbs-Merrill Company, 1971), edited by Delwin Brown, Ralph E. James, Jr., and Gene Reeves. The introduction to the latter provides the fullest history of the movement published to date. Both this volume and that edited by Cousins contain bibliographies of process theology. Articles are also to be found in the previously mentioned Hartshorne Festschrift *Process and Divinity.* More essays are contained in *Religious Experience and Process Theology: The Pastoral Concerns of a Major Modern Move-*

ment (Paulist/Newman Press, 1976), edited by Harry James Cargas and Bernard M. Lee. The April 1973 issue of the *Anglican Theological Review* (Vol. 55, No. 2) was devoted to process theology. The Spring and Fall 1975 issues of the Indianapolis-based *Encounter* (Vol. 36, Nos. 2 and 3) were also devoted to process theology.

INDEX

Actual entities: occasions, 14–15, 17–19, 81; as partially self-creative, 25–26; gradations of, 63–64; as experiencing, 77. *See also* Occasions of experience
Actuality, 14, 42; vacuous, 17
Adventure, 164. *See also* God
Agar, W. E., 174
Aim: at self-creation, 25–26; initial, 26, 29, 53, 57, 62, 73, 98, 105, 125; subjective, 26, 53, 60; at self-expression, 26–27; God's fundamental, 56, 65, 77, 121
Anaesthesia, 99, 126, 130, 140
Anselm, 44–45, 168
Aquinas, Thomas, 45–46, 52, 55, 69, 137
Arius, 108
Art, 164
Athanasius, 108
Augustine, 55, 69, 137
Axial revolution, 89

Barbour, Ian, 173, 184
Barnette, Henlee H., 183
Barth, Karl, 50, 160
Beardslee, William A., 180, 183
Beauty, 65, 83, 164
Becker, Carl, 13

Beer, Samuel H., 175
Belief(s), 85; prereflective, 30–32; as epiphenomenal, 32; conscious. *See also* Doctrine
Bera, M.A., 170
Bergson, H., 7, 169
Birch, L. Charles, 173–174
Bloch, Ernst, 83
Blyth, John W., 170
Bohm, David, 174
Bonhoeffer, Dietrich, 51
Bretall, Robert W., 178
Bright, Laurence, 173
Brown, Delwin, 184
Brown, Norman, 89
Browning, Don S., 182
Buddha, Buddhism, 39, 86, 91, 96, 137–141
Bultmann, Rudolf, 50–51, 80–84, 86, 160–161, 179
Burgers, J. M., 173

Cafaro, F., 175
Calvin, John, 52, 69
Čapek, Milic, 174
Cargas, Harry James, 185
Carothers, J. Edward, 183
Case, Shirley Jackson, 177
Cassels, Louis, 183

Causal efficacy, 154
Causation: efficient, 23, 27, 31–32, 38; final, 25–27
Cauthen, Kenneth, 173, 184
Cesselin, F., 170
Christ, 54–55, 84, 95–96, 179–181; as incarnate Logos (creative love) of God, 95, 98–101, 106; as creative transformation, 96, 102–103, 106, 131; incarnate in all things, 105–106; Jesus as, 105; and churches, 128–129
Christian, William, 171
Church, 113–114, 128–132; marks of, 106; definition of, 107; challenges for, 132, 143; and women's liberation, 132–133, 136; and Buddhism, 137–142
Clarke, Bowman, 183
Cobb, John B., Jr., 172, 178–180, 183
Collingwood, R. G., 170
Complexification, 68, 72
Complexity: and enjoyment, 64–65, 67–68, 72–73; and intensity, 64–65, 67–68; and novelty, 67–68, 73; and suffering, 72–73, 119
Concrescence, 15, 139
Concretion, principle of, 42
Consciousness, 17, 33–35, 88
Contrast, 99, 151
Cornell, George W., 183
Cousins, Ewert, 178, 182, 184
Creation, 65–66, 71
Creative synthesis, 7
Creative transformation, 100–101, 105, 131. See also Christ
Creativity, 141
Curtis, C. J., 183

Daly, Mary, 136
Das, Rashvihari, 170
Dean, William D., 183
Deism, 50

Descartes, René, 21, 76
Dewey, John, 7
Doctrine, 30–36, 39, 131; and history, 38; Buddhist, 39, 141; Christian, 39
Donne, John, 154
Douglass, James, 153
Dunkel, H. B., 174

Ecological attitude, 76
Ecological crisis, 24, 143–158
Einstein, Albert, 163
Eisendrath, C. R., 172
Ely, Stephen, 184
Emmet, Dorothy, 170
Empty space, 65–66
Enduring individuals, 65–66
Enjoyment, 16–17, 54, 57, 59, 83, 87, 146; as God's fundamental aim, 56, 65, 77, 121; and complexity, 64; involves harmony and intensity, 64, 124 (see also Intensity; Harmony); and beauty, 65
Enjuto-Bernal, Jorge, 173
Environment, 26, 27
Erikson, Erik, 182
Eslick, Leonard J., 181–182
Essence, 20
Event, 14–15, 42–43
Evil, 50, 53, 55, 69, 75, 118–119; as discord, 70, 73, 120; as unnecessary triviality, 70, 73, 120; intrinsic and instrumental, 71–72; moral, 74; temporality as, 120
Evolutionary process, 67
Existential thought, 13, 80–83
Experience, 17, 34; prereflective, 30–32, 89

Fabro, Cornelio, 184
Faith: as mode of existence, 31; as self-universalizing, 37; and historical events, 40–41

Feeling, 19–20
Felt, James W., 182
Ferré, Frederick, 183
Ferré, Nels, 166
Foley, L. A., 170
Ford, Lewis S., 169, 172
Freedom, 25, 73–74. *See also* Self-determination
Freeman, Eugene, 169
Freud, Sigmund, 17

Gentry, G. V., 170
Gilkey, Langdon, 173, 184
God, 8, 14, 21, 24, 26, 29, 41, 124, 163, 168, 184; as Cosmic Moralist, 8–9, 54–55, 58; as divine lawgiver, 8; as judge, 8; as impassible, 8–9, 44, 46, 61; as immutable, 8, 18; as Controlling Power, 9, 52–53, 55, 58, 64–65, 69, 74, 118, 156; as Sanctioner of the Status Quo, 9, 57–58; as masculine, 9–10, 61, 91, 133–135; as Divine Eros, 26, 59–61; as ground of novelty, 28–29, 59, 98, 100, 157 158; as ground of order, 28, 59–60, 72, 98; as primordial envisagement, 28, 43, 141; existence of, 41–42, 55–56; as responsive love, 44, 48, 62, 121–123; as active goodwill, 45–46, 48–49, 61; as creative love, 45–46, 48–49, 51–53, 60–61, 63, 94–95, 98, 119 (*see also* God: primordial nature of; Christ); as dipolar, 47–48, 62; as omniscient, 47–48, 52; abstract essence of, 47; actuality of, 47–48, 52, 62; primordial nature of, 48, 59, 62, 98–99, 109, 125, 135, 141–142; consequent nature of, 48, 62, 109, 122, 135, 141–142; as persuasive, 52–54, 56–57, 64, 69, 118–120, 125, 158; as source of unrest, 59; as source of chaos, 60; as source of adventure, 60–61, 75; as feminine, 61–62, 133–135; as *actus purus,* 63–64; as responsible for evil, 75; as immanent, 96–97; as incarnate in Jesus, 108–109; as nonsubstantial, 141–142; as all-inclusive experience, 151. *See also* Christ
God-relatedness, 29
Good: intrinsic, 71–72; instrumental, 71–72
Grace, divine, 35–36, 126–127, 157
Gragg, Alan, 169
Griffin, David Ray, 183
Gross, Mason W., 165

Hall, David, 175
Hamilton, Peter, 181
Hammerschmidt, W. W., 170
Hare, Peter H., 184
Harmony, 64, 183
Hartshorne, Charles, 7, 10, 43, 47, 80, 167–170, 176, 179, 183–184
Hegel, G., 7
Heidegger, Martin, 18, 80–83, 138, 160–161, 165
Heipcke, K., 173
Henry, Granville C., Jr., 175
Hepler, Cedric L., 178
Hick, John, 56
History, 84; of modes of existence, 86; and nature, 145–149; as unilinear, 152
Hitler, Adolf, 74

Ichii, S., 170
Immortality: objective, 23, 121–123; of soul, 123–124
Incarnation, 22. *See also* Christ
Independence, 21: ethical, 22
Intensity, 64–65, 75, 83
Intuition, 38

James, Ralph E., Jr., 169, 184
James, William, 172
Jaspers, Karl, 89
Jesus, 24, 40, 48, 53, 86, 96–98, 103,
    150, 160, 177, 183; his revelatory
    significance, 102, 110; his struc-
    ture of existence, 104–105; his re-
    lation to God, 104, 108–109; as
    fully human, 104, 106; as Christ,
    105; and the church, 107–108
Johnson, A. H., 166–167, 170
Jordan, Martin, 172
Jung, Carl, 134

Kant, Kantian, 77, 160–161
King, Winston, 165–166
Kingdom of heaven, 122, 141–142
Kline, George, 171
Knudson, A. C., 56

Langer, Susanne K., 164–165
Lango, J. W., 172
Language, 36–38, 84–85, 135
Laszlo, Ervin, 175
Lawrence, Nathaniel, 171–172
Leclerc, Ivor, 171, 174
Lee, Bernard M., 182
Leibniz, Gottfried, 19–21
Levi, Albert W., 172
Liberation, 25: women's, 132–136
Life, 67–68
Lineback, Richard H., 164
Locke, John, 120
Logos, 98–100. *See also* God: pri-
    mordial nature of; Christ
Lonergan, Bernard, 182
Loomer, Bernard, 178
Love: as sympathetic response, 44–
    45, 72; as active goodwill, 46; as
    persuasive, 53–54; divine (*see un-
    der* God)
Lowe, Victor, 166, 170–171
Lundeen, Lyman, 183
Luther, Martin, 52

Madden, Edward H., 184
Malik, Charles H., 165
Martin, F. David, 175
Martin, Richard M., 172
Mascall, E. L., 181, 184
Matthews, Shailer, 176–177
Mays, Wolfe, 172–173
McInerny, R. M., 181
Meland, Bernard E., 174–175, 178
Mellert, Robert B., 182
Memory, 22
Mentality, 67, 73, 164
Merleau-Ponty, Maurice, 117
Miller, D. L., 170
Miller, Randolph Crump, 179
Miracles, 49
Mitra, S. K., 176
Mohanty, J. N., 170
Monads, 20
Moral activity, 35
Morality: function of, 27; and en-
    joyment, 56–57; and adventure,
    125; and peace, 126–127; and
    mutual participation, 154–155
Moral codes, 58, 126

Neville, Robert C., 184
Niebuhr, H. Richard, 180
Niebuhr, Reinhold, 103, 180
Northrop, F. S. C., 164–165, 175
Novelty, 27–28, 59–60, 84, 101. *See
    also* God: ground of novelty
Nygren, Anders, 46

Objective datum (content), 27–28
Occasion, dominant (presiding),
    86–87
Occasions of experience, 15–17,
    19–20, 24, 28, 65, 67, 87, 101
Ogden, Schubert, 80, 82, 179
Order: and enjoyment, 59–60; so-
    cial, 60; evolution of, 64, 68, 84;
    as condition for intensity, 66; as
    mere aggregate, 78

Organism, philosophy of, 7
Origenists, 108
Orsi, C., 170
Overman, Richard, 174, 182–183

Paci, E., 173
Pailin, David A., 181
Palter, Robert M., 173–174
Parmentier, Alix, 173
Patterson, Robert E., 169
Paul, 24, 58, 81, 103, 107–108
Peace, 124–127, 140, 164
Peirce, Charles, 167
Perception, 20, 164
Perfection, 47, 52, 155; of human
    life, 21; moral, 70–71
Person, human, 137–138. *See also*
    Soul: human
Peters, Eugene H., 168, 183
Pittenger, W. Norman, 180–181
Plato, 64–65, 96–97
Pleasure, 16–17
Pols, Edward, 172
Pope, Alexander, 69
Possibility, 39, 43
Potthoff, Harvey H., 166
Prehension, 19–20
Price, Lucien, 164
Process, 7, 8, 14–15, 19, 59, 123
Proof, 36–37
Providence, 18

Rajagopal, L. V., 173
Rationality, 89–90
Realism, 7, 161
Reese, William L., 167, 169
Reeves, Gene, 184
Relatedness, essential, 19
Religion, 43, 85, 89–90
Revelation, 159
Richards, Kent H., 183
Robinson, John A. T., 181
Rust, Eric C., 184

Sacraments, 106–107
Sarkar, A. K., 170, 176
Sartre, Jean-Paul, 18
Schilling, Harold K., 173
Schilpp, Paul A., 164, 166, 170
Schleiermacher, Friedrich, 69
Schmidt, Paul F., 171
Schroeder, W. Widick, 175
Schweitzer, Albert, 76, 79
Self-determination, 24–26, 38, 71,
    73
Shahan, E. P., 170
Sherburne, Donald W., 171, 175
Simonpietri, F. A., 173
Singh, Satya Prakash, 176
Sini, C., 173
Slusser, Dorothy and Gerald, 184
Society, 15, 59; serially ordered, 15;
    democratic, 78; of mere aggre-
    gates, 78; monarchical, 87
Socrates, 86
Soleri, Paolo, 150
Soul: animal, 68, 87–88; human,
    73, 88–89; and body, 116–117
Spirit: Holy, 32, 109; human, 93.
    See also Soul
Stallknecht, N. P., 169
Stokes, Walter, 182
Structure of existence, 88–90, 116,
    160; Hindu, 90–91; Buddhist, 91;
    ethical, 91–92; Christian, 92–94,
    102; spiritual, 93–94, 102; Jesus',
    104
Subjective form, 28
Subjective immediacy, 16
Symbolism, 164
Synge, J. L., 174

Tao, Taoism, 62, 176
Teilhard de Chardin, Pierre, 18, 68,
    111–112, 115–117, 182
Temple, William, 180
Temporality, 15, 120
Theism: traditional (classical), 8,

42, 44, 47, 49, 52–53, 55–58, 61, 63–64, 69, 71, 76, 104, 108–109, 119, 121, 159; Thomistic, 42, 45–46, 167, 184; dipolar, 47, 135; process, 47, 56, 59, 62, 65, 69, 74, 76, 80–81, 118, 133, 135–141, 146, 148–150, 153, 155, 157, 159, 162–185 *passim*
Thompson, Edmund J., 169
Thompson, Kenneth F., Jr., 183
Thornton, Lionel, 180
Tillich, Paul, 51, 82
Time, 14–16
Tracy, David, 182
Transition, 14, 139
Trinity, 9, 108–110
Truth, 83, 164

Unilinear thinking, 151–154

Value: intrinsic, 16, 55–56, 59, 67, 76, 78, 121; moral, 55; in all actualities, 63, 66, 146; gradations of, 63–64, 79, 146, 148; instrumental, 67, 78–79, 121; democracy of, 147; for the whole, 150–151; ultimate, 164. *See also* Evil; Good

Waddington, C. H., 174–175
Ward, F. C., 169
Watts, Alan, 152–153
Wegener, F. C., 174
Weisenbeck, Jude D., 171
Weiss, Paul, 164–165, 167
Wells, H. K., 170
Whitehead, Alfred North, 7, 10, 12–13, 17, 29, 32–33, 36–40, 42–43, 48, 53, 59–62, 64–67, 69, 71, 78, 80–87, 95–99, 102–103, 107, 111–112, 115–117, 120–127, 130–131, 133–135, 137–142, 150–151, 154–155, 157, 160–185
Wieman, Henry Nelson, 60, 169, 177–178
Williams, Daniel Day, 178
Winquist, Charles, 182
World, 24, 144, 151, 154, 156
Wyman, Mary, 176

Zest, 111–112

30063256R10109

Made in the USA
San Bernardino, CA
04 February 2016